Praise for

EVERYDAY RESILIENCE FOR EVERYDAY HEROES

"I have a golden rule of always get back up on the horse when I take a significant wipeout in surfing. Life and surfing are similar in that you will get tossed around, and it's not always easy to find your feet or regain perspective. *Everyday Resilience for Everyday Heroes* provides simple lessons and stories to help all of us navigate our way back from those challenging times."

—Laird Hamilton
American Big-Wave Surfer

"Having been knocked down several times in my football and business career, I understand the importance of staying resilient and getting back up. In this book, Rob Clark provides a powerful framework for everyday resilience we can all appreciate. Well done, Rob!"

—Roger Staubach

"I firmly believe a loss can set you on a better path than a win, provided you have the resilience to learn from it and move forward. *Everyday Resilience for Everyday Heroes* contains uplifting stories and anecdotes to help anyone overcome their losses and get back to a winning mindset. Rob Clark has created a blueprint of positivity for any office worker, entrepreneur, parent, coach, teacher, or player."

—Morgan Wooten
Naismith Memorial Hall of Fame Coach, DeMatha High School

"At some point, everyone goes through adversity in life. It is inevitable. But it is how we react that sets us apart and can actually make us stronger. *Everyday Resilience for Everyday Heroes* offers short stories and lessons to help us turn adversity into action. And that action is the quickest path to get all of us back on the winning side."

—Lou Holtz
Hall of Fame College Football Coach

"Resilience has been the cornerstone of my life and my long coaching career. Rob Clark expertly taps into this everyday resilience with uplifting stories and lessons for all of us. I loved *Everyday Resilience for Everyday* Heroes and already can't wait for his next book."

—Charles "Lefty" Driesell
Hall of Fame Basketball Coach

"Football is like life. We all get knocked down. The question is how do you get up? Resilience. Rob Clark's book reveals the power of everyday resilience in all aspects of life."

—Michael Bidwill
Chairman and President, Arizona Cardinals

"Change brings with it transformation and reveals our true grit and ability to adapt. *Everyday Resilience for Everyday Heroes* shows us how to become stronger, wiser and better as we face inevitable change in our lives. I think the wisdom here is insightful and invaluable."

—Kristine Carlson,
NY Times Best-Selling Author, Co-author, *Don't Sweat the Small Stuff* books

"Resilience is a team sport. We can't do it alone. *Everyday Resilience for Everyday Heroes* shines light on the benefit of helping others while helping ourselves. Appreciation is a powerful force. Thank you, Rob!"

—Tom Ziglar
CEO, Ziglar, Inc. (and proud son of Zig Ziglar)

Whether we are running our own business or raising a family, we all need little reminders to deepen our appreciation and sharpen our perspective. *Everyday Resilience for Everyday Heroes* delivers relatable anecdotes and short stories to help us step back and focus on the things that truly matter."

—Daniel H. Pink
Author of *When, Drive, and To Sell Is Human*

"I have dedicated my life to helping individuals overcome adversity and increase their capacity for resilience. *Everyday Resilience for Everyday Heroes* distills many of the basic resiliency principles into an easy-to-digest, fun-to-read format. If a healthy perspective and deep appreciation is your goal, you will love this book!"

—Dr. Eva Selhub
Internationally Acclaimed Author, Speaker, and Founder, Resiliency Experts

"Rob Clark's book, *Everyday Resilience for Everyday Heroes*, provides a ray of sunlight and a message of hope to anyone who has gone through a struggle in their lives. Each story reads like a sermon and delivers a powerful lesson of resiliency for all of us. Regardless of your faith, this book will inspire you to take action and move forward with confidence."

—Monsignor John Enzler
President and CEO of Catholic Charities of the Archdiocese of Washington

"In my 2,103 days as a prisoner of war, I learned a number of life's lessons in the school of hard knocks. I lived the experience. But Rob Clark brilliantly captures the tenants of my survival in his book. He breaks down the four facets of resilience in an enjoyable and easy read for all."

—Captain Charlie Plumb
Fighter Pilot, Vietnam POW, Motivational Speaker https://charlieplumb.com

"I have dedicated my life to helping people achieve and sustain positive behavioral change. And I applaud anyone who nudges people in that same positive direction. Rob Clark is one of those people. *Everyday Resilience for Everyday Heroes* not only provides positive reinforcement, but also practical advice."

—Marshall Goldsmith
Bestselling Author and #1 Leadership Coach

"Not since Fred Astaire and Ginger Rogers exhorted us all to 'pick yourself up, dust yourself off, and start all over again' has the virtue of resilience been so eloquently expressed—until now. Make room on your dance card for Rob Clark's *Everyday Resilience for Everyday Heroes*!"

—Mo Rocca
CBS Sunday Morning Correspondent and Author of *Mobituaries: Great Lives Worth Reliving*

"Having spent time in public service, I understand the importance of resilience in keeping our country safe. Those same resilient principles apply to our personal and professional lives. Thank you, Rob, for so clearly articulating the concept of everyday resilience to keep all of us safe as well."

—Tom Ridge
First US Secretary of Homeland Security and CEO, Ridge Global

Everyday Resilience for Everyday Heroes

by Rob Clark

ISBN 978-1-64663-027-1

Published by

köehlerbooks™

3705 Shore Drive
Virginia Beach, VA 23455
800–435–4811
www.koehlerbooks.com

This book is dedicated to Reed and Phyllis Clark (aka Mom and Dad). Thank you for all the sacrifices you made for your five children. Resilience starts at the top.

EVERYDAY RESILIENCE FOR EVERYDAY HEROES

ROB CLARK

VIRGINIA BEACH
CAPE CHARLES

EVERYDAY RESILIENCE

"In three words, I can sum up everything I know about life: it goes on!"
—Robert Frost

Webster's Dictionary defines resilience as "the ability to become strong, healthy, or successful again after something bad happens." Typically, we are exposed to this concept of resilience in the superlative. We hear incredible stories of individuals overcoming major obstacles to accomplish the impossible.

The blind man who climbed Mount Everest. The scrawny little kid who blossomed into a heroic Super Bowl quarterback. The uneducated man or woman who rose up to write the Great American Novel. All these stories are motivational and remarkable. But what about the rest of us? Our stories, our struggles, our ability to persevere in the face of adversity, might not make headlines or win awards. But they require the same amount of courage and determination.

There are everyday displays of resilience taking place in classrooms, athletic fields, cubicles, corner offices, small towns, and big cities across the world. The stakes may not be as high, and the stories may not be as sensational. But summoning the courage to come back from any setback, no matter how large or small, is something to celebrate. Resilience in any form is a minor miracle!

This book shines light on the "everyday resilience" we all need to muster in our own personal and professional lives.

The ability to return from a setback stronger, healthier, and more *resilient* than ever is the key to our success and happiness. Resilient individuals do not seek out failure, disappointments, and tragedy. But they understand that these setbacks are a natural part of life and, to some degree, inevitable. Instead of retreating into a shell, resilient individuals recover and respond with *action.* Oftentimes, that action is a bold step forward to conquer new mountains!

While an upbeat outlook on life is important, there is more to resilience than simply maintaining a positive attitude. Resilient individuals need to adapt to several different types of setbacks, ranging from the difficult to the devastating. The retraction of a business. A demotion or dismissal. A damaged relationship. A failed test. A stinging defeat. A financial meltdown. The list goes on and on. But before we get too depressed, remember, we *all* have the ability to overcome these challenges and move forward with our lives!

At some point, every one of us faces some type of battle. And all of us can bounce back stronger than ever. This *everyday resilience* is perhaps the most remarkable, yet simple, power of all.

But just because it is simple does not mean that it is easy. Before we can begin, we need to recognize that resilience is a choice. We must *choose* to engage in battle. And in order to choose resilience, we first must *believe.* We must believe that we are capable, *at some point,* of achieving success and happiness. We must *believe* that our actions in the face of adversity will deliver better times in the future. We must *believe* that we can overcome our most difficult moments.

In the following pages, we will explore the four major facets of everyday resilience: *Adversity, Perspective, Passion* and *Appreciation.*

We all face **adversity** at some point in our lives. Our journey will not be a linear skyrocket to the top. There will be moments that stop us in our tracks. There will be moments that shake us to the core. But it is the ability to act and move forward *despite* the turbulent moments that defines our future success.

And during these adverse times, we need to put our setbacks in **perspective**. We are not the only ones going through a struggle. We are never alone. Focusing on the things that really matter in life (e.g., the health of our children or parents, the strength of our family, the depth of our relationships) can provide perspective and allow us to accept our smaller failures and move forward.

But nothing will happen without **passion**. And passion starts with effort. We have to fight to move forward. We have to hustle to maintain our edge. And we have to actively battle our fears to overcome any setback in our lives.

Finally, we need to maintain an **appreciation** for the people who helped us on our journey. We can't take anything for granted. Who are the people who inspire us? Who are the people who made us successful? Who are the people who protect in times of strife? Stepping away from a setback and taking the time to appreciate all our blessings will give us the strength to move forward. And appreciation will stoke the fire of our resilience.

Everyday resilience is not complex. We just need a few simple reminders to keep us on a positive track. This book serves as a handy guide to prepare us for the next challenge in our personal or professional lives. Through vignettes, quotes, and simple stories, we will cover all aspects of everyday resilience. We will lay out a game plan for everyday resilience to blossom. We will provide a blueprint for all of us to be everyday heroes!

With that kernel of optimism in mind, I invite you to take this resilient journey. I invite you to stay positive, stay strong and constantly move forward. I invite you to explore the incredible power of *everyday resilience.* Together, we will overcome adversity, maintain a proper perspective, attack our lives with passion and achieve a blissful level of appreciation.

Once we understand this, achieving everyday resilience is within reach. Anyone can do it. And it starts right now!

ADVERSITY

"Show me someone who has done something worthwhile, and I'll show you someone who has overcome adversity."
—Coach Lou Holtz

THE WIND IS ALWAYS AT OUR BACK

"May the wind always be at your back. May the sun shine warmly upon your face."
—Old Irish Blessing

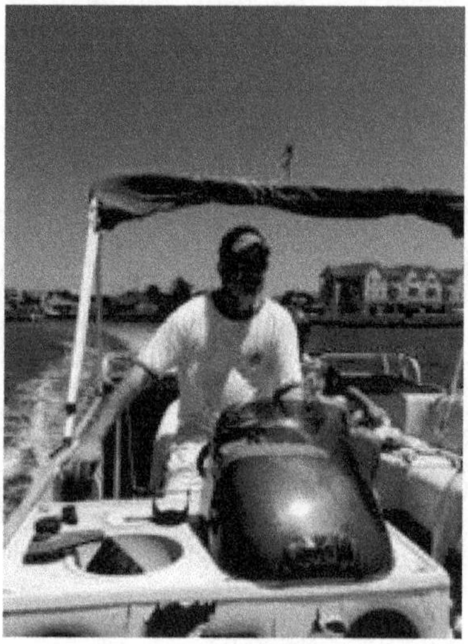

Summer is a glorious time of year, full of unique traditions and fun trips. One of my favorite getaways is to Fenwick Island, Delaware, for a weekend with a group of longtime friends. Per tradition, we always take a pontoon boat out on the water for a midday cruise around the bay. One year, as we headed north toward Bethany Beach, DE, the boat cruised effortlessly through the channel and we seemed to levitate above the water. The temperature was perfect, the sky was a brilliant azure blue, and the sun melted away all our worries. It seemed the good times would never end.

But as we turned south toward home, there was a remarkable change in conditions. The boat was fighting against the choppy waves, the temperature dropped by 20 degrees, and spray kicked up from the increasingly hostile surf. A simple reversal against the bay wind had turned a relaxing trip into a monumental struggle. As we labored toward the shore, all I wanted to do was recapture the feeling of comfort and relaxation we enjoyed just seconds ago.

In the same way, when the wind is at our back in our personal and professional lives, it seems it will last forever. Everything we do is successful, effortless and just plain fun. Relationships feel closer, work decisions feel sharper, clients are in our corner, and the feeling of optimism and accomplishment fills our lives. Everyone experiences these joyful times at some point, and they should be celebrated and appreciated.

But we must understand that the feeling may not last forever. The winds can change just as quickly, and we must be prepared to deal with the consequences. Suddenly, a friendly relationship can turn adversarial. A key decision at work can turn out to have negative consequences. Or a small tragedy in our business or personal life can suddenly impact our outlook on life. We begin to question our judgment and clarity. What was once calm and effortless is now drenched in chaos. How can we reverse course and let the wind carry us back to our happy place?

We will all experience tragedies. We will all make mistakes. We will all suffer those moments of isolation and shame. What are we going to do to reverse the wind? It is not easy, but we must recognize this is not the time to feel like a victim, give up, or curl into a ball. The world needs us to be strong!

In every tragedy or setback, there is a positive outcome we can take with us. Our relationships will be tested, but it will help us understand who will always be there for us. *Lean on these relationships!* Our business skills may fail us, but we will learn from our mistakes and become a smarter and more confident leader. *Our coworkers will support us!* If we can come back stronger from a setback or tragedy, that negative experience is actually a blessing.

How are we going to react to a sudden change in fortune? The reality is that we control the direction of the wind. If we react as if the wind is in our face all the time, we will struggle. If we recognize the wind is at our back and there is some good to come from every setback, we simply cannot lose. The choice is ours. Let's choose resilience!

Good times are ahead. Remember, the wind is always at our back!

WHEN THINGS GO BOOM!

"In any crisis, there are heroes who rise above it."
—Jerry Bruckheimer

Let's hear it for our first responders and emergency management officials! Having worked with the Federal Emergency Management Agency (FEMA) for the past ten years, I have learned firsthand the level of planning, hard work, and emotional effort that goes into keeping this country safe during a time of crisis.

And I have learned the lexicon. Emergency management officials liberally use the word "boom" in their everyday language. "Boom" can mean many things, but they are all some form of disaster. An actual *explosion*. A devastating *tornado*. A massive *hurricane*. A runaway *wildfire*. An epic *flood*. Whatever the natural or man-made tragedy, FEMA and the emergency management officials must react to "boom."

But it's not just about reaction. Obviously, the *response* to "boom" is mission critical. But what about the *preparation* for "boom"? What about the *planning* for "boom"? In order to build more stable, resilient communities, the emergency management officials need to focus on what happens "left of boom." How can we mitigate the damage of a disaster on a community? How can we prepare for the worst while focusing on the everyday tasks *before* "boom" happens?

Preparation and planning are key. But some disasters are so devastating and hit with such *incredible* force they take out even the most resilient community. "Left of boom" is important. But what happens *at and after* "boom" will determine the true resilience of a community. It's all about having a plan. And preparation can positively impact recovery.

The same is true for all of us. We need to prepare for "boom" in our own lives. That will help our recovery. But some setbacks are so devastating or hit with so little warning, we can get knocked back on our heels. What is our plan for picking up the pieces? How do we react in our *personal* and *professional* lives when things go "boom"?

In our work lives, we have to face a multitude of setbacks and challenges. A downward shift in the market. An apathetic audience. A loss of a top client. An unwinnable case. Multiple rejections and an outdated business plan. What happens at "boom" is never easy. But our preparation "left of boom" will determine our resilience "right of boom."

Have we anticipated a shrinking market and shifted our strategy? Have we been cultivating a stable of smaller clients? Have we tweaked our business plan to reflect the changing buying patterns? Have we researched potential shifts in market perceptions? The hockey stick does not extend upward exponentially forever. There will always be dips. There will always be setbacks. We need to prepare for the down moments while times are good. That will help our resilience when "boom" happens!

The same is true in our personal lives. A fractured relationship. A sudden change in financial stability. The loss of a loved one. An increased reliance on substances to get us through the day. These are setbacks we wouldn't wish on our worst enemy. But we can't always control it. At some point, "boom" happens!

How willing are we to forgive? Have we saved enough for a "rainy" day? How often do we cherish and appreciate the time with our loved ones? Can we pull ourselves out of a spiral before "rock bottom" hits? We can't *control* everything, but we can't passively sit back and wait for the inevitable. We can *mitigate* the devastating impact of "boom." A little proactivity will go a long way. *Resilience starts to the "left of boom"*!

But no matter how much we *prepare*, how much we *plan*, how much we *anticipate*, we can't fully escape the impact of "boom."

Resilience is not about just "powering through" or "sucking it up." That is too simple. There are times in our lives when we will be stopped in our tracks. We won't want to go on. We need to retreat into our shell and recover. Sometimes, resilience requires us to hit the reset button. That is okay! *But we can't stay in the fetal position forever.*

We have worked too hard to stay down for long. We have won too many battles to let a loss define us. We have more going for us than we think. We have people counting on us to deliver. It's time to rise up from the ashes. It's time to pick up the pieces to the "right of boom"! No community is immune from disaster. And none of us are bulletproof. "Boom" does not discriminate. At some point, we will all be in its path.

But just as emergency managers prepare their communities and help them stay resilient, so too do we need to protect ourselves from the challenges and setbacks that plague our personal and professional lives. *Prepare. Plan. Persevere.* And even when "boom" comes out of left field, there is nothing that will stop us from moving forward.

What will you do when things go boom?

HOCKEY STICK GROWTH VS. CHUTES AND LADDERS

"Don't be embarrassed by your failures. Learn from them and start again."
—Sir Richard Branson

Every new company dreams of achieving "hockey stick" growth in the early stages of its corporate lifecycle. This is growth that, after a short period of time, increases exponentially and infinitely into the future. Once the concept takes hold, sales skyrocket and never flatten out. There are no setbacks in product development, no internal obstacles to growth, no market saturation and no competition in the marketplace. The achievement of "hockey stick" growth is nirvana to any company seeking to dominate an entire industry.

Is this a realistic expectation of a new venture? Every business plan looks great on paper. But this is only a concept until it is battle tested in the marketplace. Once the business comes to life, there will always be unforeseen challenges. There will always be competition. There will always be obstacles to growth. The path to success for any business is not always a linear journey. We will take major strides forward that release a flood of excitement and adrenaline. But we will suffer heartbreaking setbacks that test our resolve and cause us to question our strategy and judgment. This "two steps forward, one step back" progress can be frustrating. But as long as we take the time to reflect on our missteps, correct them, and move forward with confidence, our business cannot be stopped. It will come back stronger than ever, and we can take on our next great challenge.

The same journey also applies to other aspects of our lives. Our careers have moments of great success and accomplishment that catapult us to unexpected personal gratification or financial gains. But the landscape is constantly changing, and new management or new policies can knock us back down to a lower earning potential or less fulfilling duties. How do we respond? Do we make excuses or do we fight to get back on top?

Our relationships, both business and personal, grow closer over time as we learn to trust in one another. But a simple misunderstanding or disagreement can throw everything into question. Do we break off ties immediately or hunker down and communicate through the issues? Our children can make us proud as they grow into fine young men and women. But a poor decision can launch even the well-adjusted child down a dangerous path. Do we give up on them or double down with love and attention?

If you have ever played golf, you know the thrill of breaking 100 (or 90, or 80 . . . I'll stop there). But the very next time you go out, you could shank four drives into the woods and have the worst round of your life. Are you going to throw your clubs into the pond and give up the game? (Um, rhetorical question!) The reality is that nothing in our life will skyrocket toward success forever.

It is frustrating to suffer a heartbreaking failure when everything in our lives points toward infinite success. No one expects it and we rarely see it coming. But we have to realize that every time we take a step back, it is not permanent. Adversity provides us with an opportunity to reflect, refocus and come back stronger than ever!

The sooner we realize that setbacks are a natural part of life, the sooner we can focus on getting back on track. In fact, these setbacks make us appreciate all we once had and provide us with the grit and fortitude to storm back to the top. If everything in our life were easy, where would we draw our motivation? Tasting success and happiness, and losing it, only makes us hungrier for more. We cannot wallow in self-pity!

It's time to recommit to our work and get back where we belong. We must never stop building our business! We must never stop communicating in our relationships! We must never stop loving our children!

As we go along our journey, we see that life is more like that old family board game, Chutes and Ladders. There will be times when we are so close to the top we can taste it. But one wrong move can swiftly send us back down the chute to the bottom of the board. At the same time, we could feel hopelessly behind the pack, only to hit that huge ladder and propel ourselves to heights we never thought possible.

When we are on top in our life, we need to appreciate every moment, because we never know where that next chute is lurking. When we suffer a setback, we can't despair. As long as we are willing to start over and keep trying, there is a ladder that will take us right back to the top.

If we stop trying, we can never win. Ultimately, we will come out ahead if we stay resilient, work hard, and keep a positive mental attitude. Is there any other way to play the game?

FAILURE MIGHT BE THE BEST OUTCOME

"If failure is not an option, then neither is success."
—Seth Godin

In the summer of 1991, I emerged from the cocoon of college life and launched my "brilliant" sales career. I was fortunate enough to land a job with Standard Office Supply, a small, minority-owned business in Washington, DC. There was a mini-recession going on at the time and I was thankful to be gainfully employed!

It was a true baptism-by-fire commission-based job, selling office supplies across the region to various businesses. While I had some sales experience during my college summers, I had never managed a territory or prospected beyond people I actually knew.

On the first day, Dr. Milton Morris, the co-owner of the business and a brilliant entrepreneur, handed me a small list of companies to get started. These were both private companies and government agencies who had purchased office supplies in the past. It was time to dig in. *Let's get this bread!*

But after two weeks, I had exhausted the entire list with little success. How was I supposed to survive? I went back to the source of my original leads.

"Dr. Morris, I'm afraid none of the companies you gave me want to buy right now. I guess I'm done until they change their minds."

A wry smile slowly formed across his face followed by a giant cackle.

"I have faith you will figure it out."

And with that, Dr. Morris walked away.

That was no help. What did he mean? I came to him for *answers*. Now it seemed my sales career was over before it started. But as the day wore on, I couldn't shake his expression of both exasperation and giddiness. Clearly, I was missing something *big*. And clearly it was up to me to figure it out.

Over the next few days, I studied the habits of the other salespeople. They were visiting buildings and walking floor by floor to sell office supplies. They weren't working off a predetermined list. They were hustling to *find* clients, not to cross them off a piece of paper. The incredibly obvious now dawned on me. *I had no idea what it meant to prospect!* I had failed on an epic level. And figuring it out on my own deepened my embarrassment. (Now I understood the absurdity of my conversation with Dr. Morris!) But it also deepened my resolve. *Never again!*

Dr. Morris could have lectured me. He could have condescended to me or even grown angry. But, instead, he had enough faith to let me figure it out on my own. He understood that failure is a great motivator. And it might be the best path to success.

In our work lives, we never want to fail. But sometimes we are so afraid we grasp for the nearest lifeline. We look for solutions outside ourselves and hope someone will magically give us the answer: *Surely our CEO will figure out the direction of the company. Surely my boss will remove the internal roadblocks to the sale. Surely my client will understand my pitch the first time without follow-up.*

While advice and mentoring is always welcome, sometimes we have to be our own lifeline. Sometimes, we have to figure out the path forward without help. And sometimes we have to fail in the present in order to be successful in the future. Taking control of our own destiny heightens the feeling of accomplishment. But it also intensifies the devastation of failure. And that feeling will fuel our resilience. That failure might be the best thing that ever happens to us. *Never again!*

The same is true in our personal lives. We can't always rely on others to shield us from failure. Our parents won't always be there to protect us. Our spouse may not always have the answer. Our family may have competing priorities. There is no "catcher in the rye" to save us from falling off the cliff.

And that may be a good thing. At some point, we will fail on our own. And the longer we are protected, the harder it will be to recover from that failure. It's not easy. It's hard to see those closest to us struggle. But that failure will make *everyone* stronger.

Dr. Morris could have provided me with all the answers. He could have advised me on the finer points of prospecting. But he knew the lesson would sink in much deeper if I figured it out on my own. And he knew that failure would *intensify* my competitive streak and resilience.

No one wants to look foolish. No one wants to suffer defeat and ridicule. People will tell you that failure is not an option. But if that failure *strengthens* our resolve and fuels our resilience, then failure might just be the *best* option!

CATCH A WAVE AND YOU'RE SITTING ON TOP OF THE WORLD!

"Wiping out is an underappreciated skill."
—Laird Hamilton

Surfing is a skill that is learned through trial and error. Very few of us hang a perfect ten on the first attempt. We will fall off the board. We will get knocked around. Sometimes, we are too early and we get swamped by the wave or too late and we miss the wave entirely. We get frustrated and wonder why it comes so easily to so many others. But if we keep at it, eventually everything will come together. Our timing will be perfect, the wave will be perfect, the break will be perfect and soon we will be knifing through the water like a champion. There will be no greater feeling!

But how many of us give up after the first few attempts?

If we are new to a job, and the sales do not come easily, do we quickly look for greener pastures? If we are starting our own business, and we experience initial failure, do we give up and go back to the safety of cubicle life? Sometimes we join a company and it is too early in the product cycle. Mobile advertising was "the next big thing" for ten years before the iPhone made it the *next big thing*. We need patience. Sometimes we join a company too late in the product life cycle and the market is already saturated. It is time to catch the next wave.

Nothing worthwhile comes easily. We need to push through those initial setbacks and keep moving forward. There is an incredible feeling of exhilaration and confidence waiting for us if we simply get back on that board and give it another shot.

Speaking of waves, they come in all sizes and shapes. Some look perfect at the crest, but ultimately peter out and go nowhere. Some start slowly but gather steam late in the crest and provide the perfect ride. Others have a nice initial crest but then have a second break late in the wave that packs an even greater punch.

In the same way, some relationships start off so promising only to disappoint in the end. Some partnerships initially look like they will propel our business forward, only to ultimately drag our team down. Beware of the wave that looks like it cannot lose. It might be too good to be true. Conversely, there are many relationships that start slowly but, if you give it enough time, ultimately gather steam and deliver a thrilling experience. Like surfing, it requires patience to power through the initial difficulty. Finally, how many businesses have we either joined or started that initially do well but have trouble maintaining their momentum? Stagnant markets, new competitors, and a difficult economy can challenge the long-term success of any business. Many do not have the resilience to power through to that late-breaking second wave.

Stalwart companies such as Apple, PayPal, Under Armour, and AOL each experienced initial success before plateauing with their original business models. But they were able to persevere, reinvent themselves and catch an amazing second wave of success. If we are patient and savvy, we will catch that second wave and experience a level of success we never thought possible.

Upon initial inspection, it is difficult to tell all these different waves apart. But, over time, we will begin to recognize the similarities and trends of the most successful string of waves. The perfect wave is out there waiting for us. We just have to keep looking!

The string of waves never stops rolling toward the shore. In the same way, our opportunities for success are endless. We must choose our waves wisely. And we must not fear failure. We will get knocked off our board. We will fail. But unless we get back up on that board immediately, we will never experience the sheer thrill and exhilaration of triumph through perseverance. The water is perfect. Jump on the board and ride the next wave to success and happiness!

FIND YOUR SIGNATURE LOSS

"You learn more from losing than you do from winning. A loss gets your attention and motivates you to get from where you are, to where you want to go!"
—Coach Morgan Wooten

In the sports world, struggling teams are constantly searching for that "signature win" to help put them back on the right track. A great victory against a quality opponent will allow that team to gain much-needed confidence and turn the season around. Most importantly, it will help erase the sting of the previous losses.

In the same way, there is nothing sweeter than savoring a signature win in our own lives. Perhaps a landmark deal we had been doggedly pursuing finally comes in the door. Or we hire a key resource that will help propel our business to new levels. Or a child finally breaks through and accomplishes a goal he or she was struggling with for years. All these victories are cause for celebration, and it is important to recognize and cherish these moments.

While victories are fantastic, some of the greatest teams in history turned their seasons around after a signature *loss*, not a signature win. A loss causes great teams to focus, adjust priorities, and come back stronger and hungrier for success.

But when many of us experience a loss in our business or personal lives, our natural defense mechanism kicks in to erase the painful memories. After a period of sulking, we want to move on as quickly as possible. In many ways, this is a healthy response and it is much better than curling into a ball and giving up entirely. But sometimes we can learn more from a loss than from a win.

Before moving on, it is important to analyze the reasons for our failure.

Why did we lose the big sale, and what could we have done better? Why do our expenses outpace our income and how can we correct it? Why did our relationship fall by the wayside, and how could we have handled our interactions differently? Why did we perform poorly on the test, and how can we study more effectively in the future?

Before we conquer new challenges, we must understand why we failed in the first place. This moment of honesty and introspection is not always easy, but it is one of the keys to a resilient life. A significant setback can be devastating and drain our confidence and enthusiasm. But if we stay resilient and remain open to change, a signature loss can be the catalyst we need to turn our life around.

Some of the most successful business people in the world failed multiple times before striking it rich. Henry Ford's first two car companies went belly up and left him nearly penniless. Turns out Ford Motor Company had some legs. Bill Gates' first company, Traf-O-Data, fizzled out shortly after he dropped out of Harvard. But Microsoft might just be here to stay. And last, but certainly not least, Colonel Sanders was turned down by over a thousand restaurants before he finally got it right and created the most *delicious* chicken in the world. Perseverance was only part of their story. All three of these American business titans analyzed their failures, tweaked their original ideas, and came back stronger than ever. A signature loss (or losses!) is exactly what they needed to ultimately win.

And so it is with all of us. Failure and loss are an inevitable part of life. The ability to learn from these failures and move forward defines our character and shapes our destiny. The discipline and grit required to process that loss makes us hungrier for future success.

It will not be easy. We have to muster the strength to learn from our failures and summon the intestinal fortitude to come back stronger than ever. But we can do it. Finding that signature loss might just be the greatest victory of our lives!

THE PERFECT TIME FOR IMPERFECTION

"Within every obstacle is an opportunity to improve our condition."
—Ryan Holiday

For far too long, I contemplated adding video into my weekly blog, "The Resilient Worker". It seemed a logical extension of the brand and a great way to build a more personal connection with my audience.

I researched the most effective equipment. I sketched out a few scenes. I watched how other professionals weaved in the new medium. And the more I studied it, the more I froze!

After a lot of soul-searching and internal debate, I decided it wasn't the perfect time to tinker with the formula. The quality and consistency of the blog was easy to control. Video promised new possibilities, but also introduced new complications. What if the video came out blurry? What if I couldn't master the technology? What if I looked ridiculous? The timing just didn't feel right. I wanted everything to be perfect.

But after a conversation with my sister-in-law, I realized there is no perfect time. I might end up waiting around forever! *Carpe Diem!* I prepared a few words, grabbed the old-fashioned iPhone, and broadcast my first message on Instagram.

And it was a disaster.

What I thought was the "on" button was actually the "off" button. And vice versa. My video consisted of me staring into the camera with a goofy look on my face. Followed by a cut to another shot of me looking even more clueless. And somehow it broadcast out to my audience. *D'oh!*

While my kids got a HUGE laugh at my expense, it didn't exactly enhance my brand. It was, to say the least, incredibly imperfect. And yet it was a start. It created momentum. And it provided an opportunity to improve. Most importantly, it *increased* my conviction and dedication to branch into a new area. In the end, this imperfection was the BEST thing that could have happened to me. Because it was a step forward.

It was the perfect moment for imperfection. And that is good perspective to embrace for our work and personal lives.

In our work lives, it is easy to sit back and wait for the *perfect* time to execute. But that moment may never come. Managers don't always have the luxury of waiting for the "perfect" job candidate. Entrepreneurs can't always wait for the "perfect" business conditions. Salespeople can't always hold out for the "perfect" deal. Sometimes, waiting for "perfect" will stifle our momentum. Because "perfect" is elusive.

Job candidates can quickly disappear. Business conditions can rapidly change. Deal terms are in constant flux. Waiting for perfect can lead to paralysis. Building the airplane while we fly is not ideal. But it's better than spending our whole life on the ground. Sometimes, we just have to dive in with both feet and have a little faith!

The same is true in our personal lives. There is no "perfect" time to ask someone out or start our families. There is no "perfect" time to start exercising. We can't write the "perfect" article without writing a lot of subpar ones. We can't improve in any sport or skill unless we actually take that first step and *do* something. We may not be perfect right out of the gates, but we need to *start* the journey.

And *starting* is the most important step. It doesn't have to be a thing of beauty. It might even cause us embarrassment and ridicule. But we have to get comfortable with being uncomfortable. Shaking off stagnation and actually *doing* something will put us on a path toward success. Even if our first step is a failure.

I am not suggesting we settle. I am not suggesting we accept mediocrity and learn to appreciate failure. While action is important, it shouldn't come at the expense of preparation and caution. We shouldn't just blindly dive into something without some basic understanding of the outcome.

But we can't run models forever. We can't *plan* forever. We can't *think about* our dreams forever. Analysis in the absence of action is certain paralysis. At some point we need to actually take that first step forward. Even if that first step is the essence of imperfection.

We all have special talents. We all have some calling or vocation. We all have goals and dreams in our personal and professional lives. But those dreams can't just lurk *within* us. We have to *take action* to realize any level of success or fulfillment. And we have to accept the fact that the first steps may come with pain and heartache.

Resilience starts and ends with action. We can't retreat back into the shell at our first sign of adversity. We have to keep the faith. Imperfection is not the enemy of success. Only *inaction*.

We can't get better unless we act. So why wait another day? Now is the perfect time.

AT SOME POINT, EVERYONE NEEDS THEIR GHEE-GHEE

"Cure sometimes, treat often, comfort always."
—Hippocrates

Most of us had some special blanket, stuffed animal or pillow that we caressed in our crib and coddled through our early childhood years. (Some held on longer than others!) They come in different shapes and sizes and they go by different names. For my children, it was, in order, *Froggy, Bunny, Taggy,* and *Puppy.* And I had a cousin who carried around his stuffed bear named Ghee-Ghee all the way through college. *No judgement!*

Regardless of the names, they all served one basic purpose: comfort. When we were tired, frustrated, furious, lonely, bored, scared, or sad, our "Ghee-Ghee" got us through the difficult times. It seemed we could never go on without it.

But, at some point, we all outgrew our reliance on this comfort. At some point, we had to fend for ourselves and take on the world without our crutch. This is healthy, shows growth, and is a natural part of the maturation process. But no matter how old and resolute we become, there are still times when we need the soothing comfort of our Ghee-Ghee!

Professionally, we all hit a rut or a streak of poor performance that causes us to question our abilities. We lose confidence and think our best work is behind us. Perhaps we have lost a case. Perhaps we have lost a client or a sale. Perhaps we can no longer connect with our students or our players. How do we pick up the pieces and move on? The best way to move forward and stay resilient is to hearken back to the one area in which we are naturally gifted. The one area where success comes easily for us. This is our Ghee-Ghee!

If you are a visual learner, create graphics to help you study for the next test. If you are more comfortable with research than courtroom trial, focus on building your next case in the library. If you are socially gifted and adept at building relationships, focus on scheduling a lunch or social function with a new client. If you teach or coach, perhaps finding innovative methods to impact the lives of your students or players has always come naturally to you. Focus on your next innovation and get your mojo back. The only way to recover from the difficult times is through action. We all must recognize the natural gift that will get us moving in the right direction.

In our personal lives, there are times when we need similar comfort. A broken heart. A broken dream. Disillusionment with a previously held ideal. What will allow us to feel better and move on? Perhaps watching a sunset. Taking a long run. Putting our feet in the ocean. Or just having a talk with Mom. Whatever it is, we need to make it easy on ourselves. When moving forward seems impossible, we must find our security blanket and channel our inner Ghee-Ghee!

But we can't solely concentrate on this special talent or security blanket to carry us for the rest of our lives. There is a danger in getting *too* comfortable in our comfort zone. At some point, we need to move on and try things that makes us *uncomfortable*. In fact, success often comes from developing skills in something that does *not* come naturally to us.

But in times of crisis, we need to get "unstuck." In times of crisis, we need to take action. If finding comfort helps us take that first step forward, let's go for it! If finding comfort helps restore our confidence, let's make it happen.

We never truly outgrow our need for occasional security, comfort, and peace of mind. The objects may change. The people may change. The methods may change. But we all need to return to that place of warmth at some point in our lives. Don't be afraid to seek this out in times of despair. As long as it is not physically or emotionally damaging, this security blanket can help us maintain our resilience.

But we cannot spend our life in this place. Once we have restored our balance, we must go out and seek our next great adventure. We must go out and conquer our next great challenge! And if we stumble again, there is no need to worry.

Our Ghee-Ghee will always be there for us!

EMBRACE THE MONSTER!

"Courage is the willingness to act in spite of fear."
—Michael Hyatt

Is there anything better than the family beach vacation? Sun. Sand. Surf. Spikeball. *Extended happy hours.* All our minor troubles seem to disappear in the salt air and suntan lotion.

But when my youngest daughter, Cassidy, was seven years old, our trip to the beach entailed staring down a *monster.*

She desperately wanted to use the boogie board but couldn't get past the first set of smaller waves. She would sprint through the shallow surf but then abruptly turn and run toward the safety of the shore just before the tiny wave crashed.

Every time she ran away, the waves grew more menacing in her mind. Before too long, running away became a habit. Normally tough-minded and focused, she was now allowing the monster of the ocean to dictate her plans and crush her goals.

After a few hours of struggle, and some *family encouragement,* she *finally* changed her mindset. Rather than running away, she realized *attacking* the wave was the best way to overcome her fears. Once she confronted the waves, they no longer seemed so frightening. And it opened a whole new world of fun and excitement she never thought possible. *Time to hang ten!*

And we all face similar monsters in our work and personal lives. The sooner we confront them, the sooner we can tackle all our goals and dreams.

In our work lives, we have fears and insecurities we need to overcome. We can try to ignore them or create coping mechanisms to minimize their impact. But we will never truly reach our potential until we face them head-on. And the longer we run from them, the more terrifying they become in our mind. Dealing with a painful client. Making a difficult decision on personnel or a player who is hurting the team. Taking the first step toward writing a business plan. Starting the Great American Novel. Asking for that promotion. Making cold calls to grow the business. All of these entail staring down the monster.

On that last point, an old boss, Pete Briskman, once offered me some simple advice to help me overcome my own fears:

"If you are afraid of making cold calls, I have the perfect solution. Make cold calls!"

It took me a while to process, but it is so true. The only way to overcome our fears is to dive right into the wave and start kicking!

We can tell ourselves we will do it tomorrow. We can convince ourselves we can live without it. We can pretend we don't need to do it. But deep down, we know those are subtle lies. And the longer we try to lock our monsters in the closet, the louder and more hideous they become.

The same is true in our personal lives. The longer we wait to exercise, the harder it is to take that first step toward better health. The longer we wait to repair a strained family relationship, the greater the chance we lose touch entirely. The longer we wait to address our financial situation, the deeper the hole becomes.

Our monsters will only grow more powerful if we continue to ignore them. Our most difficult challenges will not just go away. They are holding us back more than we will ever know.

We need to act *today*! It's time to run toward the waves and plunge right in.

But what happens when we dive in and get tossed around like a rag doll? What happens when our monsters bite back?

Our client rips into us. We ask for the promotion and get turned down. We make cold calls and get rejected. We try to repair a relationship and it uncovers deep-seated resentment. We try to save money but the financial hole grows deeper.

That is okay. If we fail while boldly facing our fears, we can never lose in the long run. Even if the monster wins the initial *battle*, we now see that this is a *war* we can win! By facing our monsters head-on, our courage will help diminish our deepest fears.

Courage is a muscle. The more we exercise it, especially in the face of adversity, the stronger we become. And even if we do not come out on top, our courage helps us see that the monster is not so scary. Now we know that we can *eventually* beat them down.

We are not going to win every battle. We are never going to go undefeated. But if we demonstrate the *courage* to tackle our challenges head-on, we will win in the end.

The small waves turn into tsunamis if we run away. Our blind spots and fears will slowly erode our dreams if we choose to ignore them. Our monsters only grow more powerful if we try to lock them up.

It is not going to be easy. It will take hard work. It will take incredible discipline. But most of all, achieving success and happiness will take the *uncommon courage* to face our fears.

Embrace the monster. Dive into the next wave. Watch all your dreams come true!

YOU CAN'T ALWAYS PLAY IT DOWN THE MIDDLE

"I don't believe in taking foolish chances, but nothing worthwhile can be accomplished without taking any chances at all."
—Charles Lindbergh

There is a time and place to play it safe in life. It doesn't always make sense to take a risky path in business and jeopardize the security of our family. Sometimes, it is difficult to take a politically unpopular stance if it means risking our careers. There are times we need to be diplomatic and stifle our true emotions for the greater good of the company or to spare the feelings of those in our inner circle. Playing it down the middle is the perfect plan for golf. And sometimes it is a necessary and prudent move in our adult lives. *Sometimes.*

But if we want to live a resilient life, we cannot make a habit out of playing it down the middle. There are times when we must throw all caution to the wind and steadfastly believe in our own abilities.

It may not make immediate financial sense to start our own business. But if we have the right idea and a burning passion to branch out, we need to take that risk. As a manager, it may be safe to hire the candidate who looks good on paper. But sometimes we have to take a risk on the candidate that just feels right in our gut. When hiring a vendor, it is usually safer to bring on the larger company with a proven track record. But there are scrappier companies with enormous upside who could turn our business around if we are willing to take the risk.

In our personal lives, sometimes we may have to defend someone who is unpopular or an easy target. We may risk losing social capital, but if defending this person feels right, why stay silent? For every reason there is to play it safe, we can make a counter-argument to risk it all. So what are we supposed to do?

This is a difficult and nuanced question, and no one can provide a definitive answer. But generally, it comes down to simple math. We know that by taking enough risks, we are bound to fail at some point. Taking risks has been romanticized throughout history as the ultimate expression of bravado and a sure-fire path to success. But taking a risk is, well, *risky*, and it can come with an unbearable downside. This failure can be painful and traumatic and should not be trivialized.

But with the right attitude, we can overcome these setbacks and prepare ourselves for our next great plan. If we keep moving forward, we can learn from our mistakes and greatly increase our chances of future success. The odds are now in our favor.

Conversely, if we *never* take risks in either our careers or personal life, we may spare ourselves from the stinging pain of defeat or failure. But we will never experience the *unbridled joy* of conquering our fears and pushing ourselves to achieve incredible success.

Playing it down the middle *all the time* ensures a life somewhere in purgatory. No great pain, *yet no great joy.* No financial hardship, *yet no long-term financial boon.* No excruciating broken heart, *yet no passionate love.* Playing it down the middle all the time is more likely to lead to an unfulfilled life destined for mediocrity. That math simply does not work.

One last word about risk. I am not suggesting we take foolish risks in the fruitless search for our next adrenaline rush. While I was a *huge* Evel Knievel fan as a child, I am not talking about performing outlandish physical stunts or engaging in risky and destructive social behavior. I am referring to risks designed to improve our quality of life and our self-esteem. Our risks should be calculated based on our perceptions in the moment. We need to trust our instincts! We need to listen to the little voice inside our head that wants us to succeed! We need to let passion be our guide!

We know it won't be easy. We know there will be struggles. But we also know that we can never achieve greatness by always playing life down the middle.

THE BIG CAT WALKS LATE

"A smooth sea never made a skillful mariner."
—English Proverb

There is a saying in poker (at least in my poker group) that has special meaning for everyday resilience: "The big cat walks late."

What exactly does this mean?

There will be times, early in the night of poker, when fortune may not be smiling upon us. Despite great strategy and decent cards, we may not win a single hand. Our frustration mounts as our chips dwindle. But we must not lose our optimism! We must not lose our focus! It's not how we start; it's about how we finish. Inevitably, the early round losers who have the wherewithal to persevere end up as big winners by the end of the evening. The night is a marathon, not a sprint, and those early losses only strengthen our resolve as the rounds roll on.

Conversely, amassing early wins can take away our edge. The victories pile up, and it may feel as if the streak is going to last forever. Oftentimes, the early winners fizzle out in the end and go home disappointed and disillusioned. We must maintain our resolve if we are going to stay on top. Everyone wants to take a shot at knocking down the early chip leader. If the wins are coming too easily, our pile becomes harder to defend. Anyone can have success early. But only the big cat walks late!

The same is true in our professional lives. It can be a struggle in the early part of our career. We may be too young and not taken seriously. We may make a critical mistake due to our lack of experience. Some of our early business ventures may fail entirely. But we need to maintain our enthusiasm and focus during these difficult times. There will be setbacks. There will be heartaches. But as long as we are moving forward, we can solve these problems and learn from our mistakes. If we are staying positive, we can withstand those early defeats and discover our true potential.

No matter where we are on the spectrum of life, there is always an opportunity to realize our dreams. The only way we can lose is if we fold our cards and go home. The only way we can lose is if we believe our best days are behind us. As long as we stay positive, and maintain our effort, we will see our chip stack grow and our victories pile up. And those early losses will allow us to appreciate our victories even more. Our resilience and ability to move forward in the face of defeat will define our life. Nothing will be able to stop us. The big cat *will* walk late!

Not to say there is anything inherently wrong with early success. Some people live a charmed life. They start off strong and they finish strong in business and in life. There are times when the big cat walks early AND late. God bless them, and I wish those people continued happiness.

Failure is not a prerequisite for success. But it is more difficult to appreciate our victories if success is all we have ever known. It is more difficult to maintain our resilience if we have never faced adversity. Nobody sets out to fail. Nobody wants to suffer misfortune or heartache. Nobody seeks out roadblocks in their life. But our early losses play a huge role in forming our character. Our early adversity provides us with the determination to propel us back to the top. Once we get there, those early defeats will give us the confidence to *stay* on top. And what a sweet journey that will be!

Not everything will be easy. Especially in the beginning. But it's all about how we finish. A student may struggle early in grade school only to emerge as an honors scholar in college. An athlete may struggle with coordination and confidence as a child only to emerge as a star player in high school or college. An entrepreneur may endure several failed businesses before founding the next Fortune 500 behemoth.

Perhaps we are a late bloomer. Perhaps we have not found our true calling. Perhaps we simply have not found the right opportunity. We are too smart and too talented to fail in the long run.

Stay resilient! Stay positive! Stay motivated! We may stumble early in the journey, but we need to keep moving forward into the later rounds. We are the Big Cat. And the Big Cat walks late!

FREE WILL AND THE POWER OF CHOICE

"Fate is the hand of cards we've been dealt. Choice is how we play the hand."
—Marshall Goldsmith

One of the greatest blessings in our life is free will. Think about it. We wake up in the morning and have the freedom to do whatever we want that day. With the major responsibilities in our lives, it may not always feel that way, but it is true. On a daily basis, there is no one telling us what to do and no script we have to follow. The day is our canvas, and we have the choice to apply as much or as little paint as we wish. This day, this week, this month, this year, this life is what we make of it.

We can get up early, exercise, attack the day and get a jump start on our lives. Or we can sleep in and play video games all day. No matter what choices we make, those choices are ours and we have to own them!

We have free will, but we must recognize that our choices also have consequences. Fortunately, most of us have a built-in control mechanism that factors in our responsibilities. Skip work and head off to the beach? We might lose out on much-needed revenue. Blow off class and hit the mall? Our grades might suffer as a result. Go to the spa instead of paying the bills? We might soon be operating in the red.

Our free will is a blessing, but it also comes with a potentially destructive downside if we abuse it. What can help us down the right path? A strong work ethic. A solid moral base. A supportive family or close friends who share our same values. Free will left unchecked can be damaging. But free will surrounded by positive influences and positive intentions can be incredibly powerful. Given the right guidance, we can accomplish anything.

Want to start your own company? No one is stopping you. Want to play the piano? You can find the time. Want to write a story? It starts with the first sentence. With the right attitude and encouragement, success becomes a choice. Our potential is unlimited. Never underestimate the power of free will.

But what does free will have to do with adversity and everyday resilience? When we suffer a setback or make a major mistake in our lives, there is no playbook. This can be painful, and sometimes it feels as if success will never come our way. We can choose to retreat into a shell and feel sorry for ourselves. We can choose to blame others for our own problems. We can choose to play it safe and refuse to take any more risks. Or we can *choose* resilience.

It takes incredible determination to launch our next business venture after a failure. It takes incredible courage to forgive ourselves and turn the page after a major mistake. It takes incredible effort to still try our hardest in the face of certain defeat. Resilience is not easy. But resilience is a choice. And it comes with such a huge upside if we can muster the grit to move forward.

We will come back stronger than we were before the setback. We will appreciate the things we may have taken for granted. We will be hungrier for success and happiness the next time we experience a difficult situation. No one can be resilient for us. We must make that *choice* on our own.

Nothing is predetermined in our lives. Our decisions and attitude will determine whether our setback was a blip on the radar or a harbinger of doom for things to come. We need to make the most of our God-given gift of free will. The decisions we make after a setback will set us on a path toward success or failure. Do we want to give up, or do we want to move forward stronger than ever? The choice is ours!

SOMETIMES, WALKING AWAY IS THE BEST OPTION

"Being able to quit things that don't work is integral to being a winner."
—Tim Ferriss

Let's face it. Life is not designed for the weak. Often, our greatest accomplishments develop from struggle and perseverance. There are so many times we need to dig deep, stay positive and keep on moving forward. If we are able to break through the down moments without giving up, we can glean an even greater appreciation for our accomplishments. It is this adversity that forms our character and gives us the strength to treasure our life and pass on our hard-fought lessons to the next generation. But everyone has a breaking point. How do we decide when enough is enough?

In our work life, we need to perform overwhelming tasks and power through difficult moments of doubt and uncertainty. A strategic merger which leaves us with overlapping job responsibilities. A new boss who does not value our expertise. The loss of a major client or sale. A massive dip in the stock. All of these can knock us back on our heels and cause a loss of confidence and conviction. Our ability to bounce back is driven by our inner fortitude and resilience. Most of the time, we will be a phoenix rising from the ashes!

But there are difficult moments that transcend resilience. What happens when we are asked to do something that conflicts with our beliefs or morals? What happens when our misery at work bleeds into our family and personal life? What happens when our health starts to suffer from the stress and anxiety brought on in the workplace? As important as it is to persevere and overcome adversity, it is even more important to take care of our health, take care of our family and stay true to our moral compass. Sometimes, we have to say enough is enough and walk away.

In our personal life, everyday resilience is a crucial asset. We may get cut from a sports team, suffer a setback in a relationship, experience financial hardship, or feel out of place in our school or social life. Once again, a positive attitude and the conviction that we are not alone can fuel our resilience in these difficult moments. We must fight through the urge to give up, and tap into our inner strength and positive attitude. We are too strong to stay down forever!

But what happens when we do everything we can to impress a coach, and he still does not take notice? What happens when we work as hard as possible, but the bills keep on coming? What happens when we keep trying to branch out and make connections, but our isolation only gets more prominent? There are times when we need to take a deep breath and pause before continuing down the same, tired path. A change of scenery may be necessary in order to stay resilient for another day.

Sometimes, it is okay to walk away from a job. Sometimes, it is okay to walk away from a relationship. Sometimes it is okay to walk away from our current social scene. Sometimes, it is okay to downsize our life until the storm passes. Nobody ever said life was supposed to be easy. But it isn't supposed to be an endless grind! We are far too valuable to spend our life in desperation.

There are people in our life who need us. We cannot allow our health to suffer. We cannot allow ourselves to become sad, bitter or self-focused. We cannot wallow in self-pity. When a situation turns unhealthy or unbearable, we must understand that we have options. And sometimes the best option is to quit embracing the madness and simply move on.

What is that breaking point? The reality is that the threshold is different for every person. But it is always *well beyond* our initial feeling of discomfort. If we give up too easily, we will never be able to sharpen our character and appreciate our accomplishments. If we give up too easily, we will never experience the unbridled joy that stems from staring down our demons. If we give up too easily, we will never know the power of everyday resilience.

But there is a fine line between everyday resilience and insanity. It is not a badge of honor to endure senseless pain. There are times we must decide that enough is enough.

Everyday heroes know that sometimes it takes more courage to walk away from a dysfunctional situation than to head down the same fruitless path. And if we decide to walk away, we need to put a smile on our face, move forward with confidence, and never look back with regret.

EVERYDAY RESILIENCE PROFILE ON ADVERSITY: MEET TIM STRACHAN

Tim "T." Strachan had a simple but powerful dream. Ever since he was five years old, he wanted to play college football. This was not a whimsical fantasy. He was passionate about his goal. He was dedicated to the cause. And he had the drive and the athletic ability to make his dream a reality!

As the youngest of four brothers, he also had the benefit of emulating the athletic accomplishments of his older siblings. Armed with this foundation, T. Strachan *dominated* as a gun-slinging quarterback in youth football. His legend grew. When the decision came to attend high school, he fell in love with DeMatha High School and enrolled there in the fall of 1990.

Turning the Dream into Reality

While football was his passion, T. Strachan also excelled on the basketball court and had the opportunity to play for legendary DeMatha basketball coach Morgan Wootten. It was under Coach Wootten that Strachan fully grasped the potential of his athletic ability. And, more importantly, he learned the significance of perspective and appreciating his present situation. Coach Wooten reminded him this was a special time in his life and encouraged him to *enjoy every moment.*

Armed with this healthy outlook, T. Strachan channeled his raw athletic ability into the game of football. He learned the system his freshmen year as a backup quarterback. But halfway through his second season, Strachan got his shot at glory. And he led DeMatha on a late-season surge that culminated with a Washington Catholic Athletic Conference (WCAC) Championship!

Strachan's junior season was even more impressive. Led by their 6'3", 225-pound quarterback, DeMatha rolled through the competition and captured their second consecutive WCAC Championship. By this time T. Strachan was on the radar of every major college football coach on the East Coast.

In the summer before his senior season, Strachan was living his dream. The Pre-Season High School All-American team came out, and T. Strachan was listed as one of the top five quarterbacks in the country (along with another *slightly* successful quarterback—Peyton Manning!). Three days later, Strachan received an invitation to meet legendary Penn State football coach Joe Paterno. Coach Paterno offered him a *full scholarship* to play college football at Penn State University. It would not be his last offer.

The dream was within his grasp.

Tragedy Strikes

August 5, 1993—just a few weeks before the start of T.'s senior-year football camp. It was a beautiful day in Bethany Beach, Delaware, and the entire Strachan family was gathered on the beach. T. was enjoying a friendly (yet competitive) beach volleyball game. He had worked up a sweat and needed to cool off. So he sprinted toward the ocean and dove into a large wave just before it crashed onto shore.

Suddenly, everything changed.

T. could not feel his legs. His family rushed in and turned him over. He had fractured the C-5 vertebrae in his neck. It did not look good.

He was immediately medivacked to a hospital in Philadelphia where he would endure two major surgeries over a nineteen-hour period. T. was in and out of consciousness over the next few days. On the third day, he awoke and asked the nurse when he would be able to play football again.

The nurse hesitated. She did not want to be the one to tell T. Strachan he would never walk again.

Shortly thereafter, T.'s father came into the hospital room. His son was dealing was the severity of the nightmare unfolding before him. What do you say to someone you love in that incredibly vulnerable and delicate moment?

"Son, you're not going to be able to do the things you used to do. But you're still T. You'll always be T!"

That gave T. Strachan the strength he needed to move forward with his new reality. The dream of playing college football had vanished.

But he was still the same person he was before the accident. He was still T. He would always be T.

Settling into a New Reality

Real life is not like the movies. Rarely is there a cathartic moment followed by a linear journey back to the top. A tragedy is a tragedy, and T. still struggled at times with his new reality. He had some bad days over the next three months in the ICU. He grew frustrated with his constant physical therapy and subsequent surgeries. He could not help but think of his teammates as they took the field to capture another title.

His peers would be moving on without him. The world did not stop.

But he had the unwavering support of his loving family. He had over fifty visitors a day in the hospital. He had the backing of the entire community. He was never alone. And that gave him the strength to move forward.

New Dreams Emerge

Joe Paterno still honored T.'s scholarship at Penn State. But Coach Duffner had also offered a scholarship to the University of Maryland, and T. needed to be closer to family.

In the fall of 1996, T. Strachan enrolled at the University of Maryland. It was then that he received his first major break. Family friend and legendary announcer Johnny Holliday offered T. a position as a sideline reporter for the home University of Maryland football games. He had no experience. It was a trial by fire. But like most things in his life, he attacked it with passion and soon hit his stride.

Public speaking did not come naturally to T. But he was driven to be the best and soon realized this would be a critical skill moving forward. He linked up with Dr. Leah Waks, a professor at UMD for the Department of Communication. This would eventually become his major. And it was a skill that would serve him well. (Ten years later, T. would be the student keynote speaker at the University of Maryland Communications Department graduation ceremony.)

After graduation, a friend and mentor, Bob Muse, convinced T. to attend law school. Once again, he hunkered down in his studies at Georgetown University Law Center and graduated with honors. He eventually took the position of counsel to the Senate Judiciary Committee. The sky was the limit.

But to top it all off, during his first year at law school, Strachan was reunited with Leslie, the girl he had "gone steady with" in second grade. It didn't take long to rekindle the past. They were married in the fall of 2005.

There Is No End to the Dream

Today, T. Strachan is celebrating his twenty-fourth year as a broadcaster for the University of Maryland. He also accepted a promotion at the Federal Communications Commission as the acting director of Legislative Affairs. He and Leslie have two beautiful daughters, Sophie and Olivia.

In addition, along with partners Kevin Ricca and Ken Meringolo, he launched a podcast ("1stAmendmentSports") which streams live high school games and content and has a hyper-local focus on the professional landscape of Washington, DC, sports. And in between the demands of his burgeoning career and family life, he finds the time to deliver motivational speeches and host charity events.

T. Strachan had a dream to be a college football player. That did not happen.

But did he ever dream he could be a dynamic public speaker?

Did he ever dream he would spend twenty-four years as a broadcaster?

Did he ever dream he would attend law school?

Did he ever dream he would hold a job with this much responsibility?

Did he ever dream he would marry his grade-school sweetheart?

Did he ever dream he would have two precious daughters?

Did he ever dream he would have such an impact on his community?

T. Strachan stayed resilient. **Only one dream ended.** But a lifetime of dreams ensued.

What Does It Mean for Us?

T. Strachan's story can teach us many lessons. The significance of friends and family in our journey. The importance of staying resilient and constantly moving forward. The impact of hard work and dedication to a goal.

But most importantly, T. Strachan can teach us about **the simple power of pursuing a dream**. We don't have control of a lot of things in our life. The road can get bumpy and adversity can strike at any time. But we can control our focus and we can control our dreams.

And once we summon the passion and focus to attack one dream, it opens the possibility for so many more!

We aren't always going to be successful. But that can never stop us from pushing forward toward our goal. If one dream ends, another will be there to take its place. And it might be better than our original dream.

What is your dream? It doesn't have to change the world. But we all need one. *And once we identify it, we must own it!*

Dreams feed our energy. Dreams give us hope for the future. Dreams inspire all those around us.

*And, one way or another, our dreams **will** come true.*

T. Strachan is living his dream. And so will you!

PERSPECTIVE

"Every single person has a different perspective when looking at the same thing."
—Edward Huang

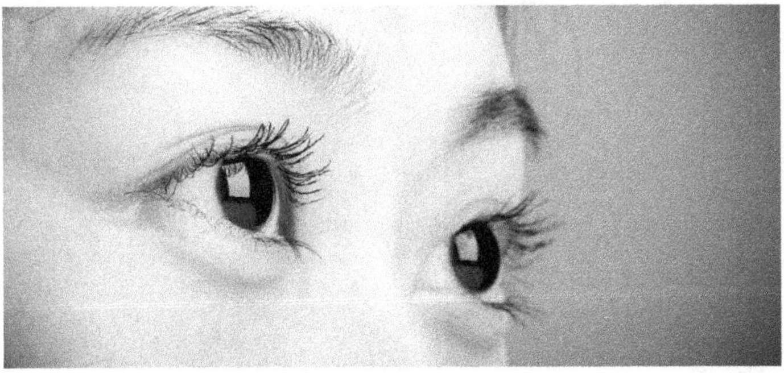

IT'S ALL A MATTER OF PERSPECTIVE

"The only thing you have control over is perspective. You don't have control over your situation. But you have a choice about how you view it."
—Chris Pine

Sometimes, perspective hits you over the head like a bucket of ice-cold water.

I was with a colleague on Capitol Hill in Washington, DC, a few years back, visiting policy-makers and gathering information for my clients. In our final meeting of the day, we received some news that could negatively impact our biggest customer. I could feel my stomach turn and my chest constrict.

We both trudged out of the meeting with our heads down. Silently, we waited for a cab as we painfully absorbed the bad news.

Suddenly, a taxi pulled up and a booming voice bellowed out from inside.

"Welcome, my friends!"

Oh, boy. This guy was WAY too happy.

We piled into the back and slumped into our seats.

"My friends, why do you look so sad?"

Just drive the cab, buddy.

"Is it your health? Perhaps your family?"

What is this, twenty questions? C'mon!

Finally, I broke the silence. I begrudgingly explained the disastrous meeting. The cabbie listened intently and then broke into a giant smile.

Was he making fun of us?

"My friends, I am from Sierra Leone. As you know, we have endured many atrocities in our country. Sometimes, it seems impossible to go on. But we have a saying that keeps us moving forward: ***Don't complain about your shoes, when your neighbor has no feet!"***

Splash! Ice bucket challenge in the back of a DC taxi!

Our everyday lives can become overwhelming. We have massive financial responsibilities. We have to preserve the family structure. We have people counting on us to perform. We have to meet the emotional needs of our close friends and family members. With so much on the line, we can quickly lose our perspective. And the smallest setbacks can have an inverse impact on our self-worth and self-esteem. A bad meeting. A lost client. A failed test. A missed market opportunity. A blown assignment. A lapse in judgement. A failure to execute. A broken relationship. A stinging defeat.

These moments are raw and they are real. But are they permanent? Are they catastrophic? Do they define us? Of course not!

With the proper perspective, we become immune from the general churn of the day. We can see hope in the face of despair.

Defeat is temporary. Failure is a moment in time, not a destination. Relationships break and then they mend. We can't let these temporary setbacks dictate our success and happiness.

With so much going for us, we can't let one bad meeting ruin our day.

Think of all the buckets we must fill in our life. Family. Friends. Work. School. Social. Athletics. Hobbies. Relationships. There is a lot to juggle. But which buckets must we prioritize? That will help determine where we focus our time and energy.

If our work bucket is full but our family bucket is dry, what is the point? If our hobby bucket is full, but our friend bucket is dry, where is the joy? We must constantly prioritize the things that truly matter in our lives. If we lose that perspective, then it is easy to drift from one destination to the next.

Without those priorities firmly established, the little things can knock us even further off course. We can all use reminders to help reset our priorities and get back on track. Inspiration can come from anywhere. Even a taxi ride.

It's time to wake up! Sometimes, a bucket of ice-cold water is exactly what we need.

But we have to be careful about completely ignoring the other buckets. Family and relationships are key. But we can't blow off our responsibilities at work. We can't stop studying for our exams. We can't dismiss our clients, abandon our coworkers, and let down our classmates. Perspective is crucial, but we still need to get stuff done!

Our day-to-day execution still matters. Perspective doesn't give us an excuse to take our eye off the ball. We will still face frustration and turmoil. We will still face a *roller coaster* of good news and bad news in our everyday lives. It is part of the journey, and some days will be better than others.

But perspective allows us to smooth out the hills and turns. Perspective allows us to stretch beyond our immediate roadblocks. Perspective allows us to ride out difficult moments and see the greater purpose in our lives.

We can't let the everyday grind extinguish our will to succeed. We can't let temporary losses define our happiness. If we are to stay resilient, we must keep our priorities straight.

Health, family, friends, relationships. Do we have those in place? If so, we can summon the strength to keep battling. If so, what do we really have to complain about?

Our shoes may be scuffed up and dirty, but our feet are firmly planted on the ground.

EVERY THORN HAS ITS ROSE

"We can complain because rose bushes have thorns, or rejoice because thorns have roses."
—Alphonse Karr

Many years ago, I was a *decent* high school running back on a *great* high school football team. I competed hard for the starting position and left it all on the field. But ultimately I ended up in a *backup* role on offense.

While I was disappointed, our team dominated every opponent, and we were having fun marching toward a perfect record. Why complain?

But in the second to last game of the season, our starting running back went down with a devastating shoulder injury. It was clear he wouldn't be returning to the game. This was my time to shine!

I *made the most of my minutes* and had a great game *en route* to another lopsided victory. The final game of the season was more of the same. It was a glorious end to a perfect season. (Cue "Glory Days.")

But I had a choice to make about how I perceived my final season of football.

I could have lamented all the wasted opportunities to showcase my talent on the field. I could have turned a positive into a negative.

What if I had started from the beginning of the season? I could have set records. I could have piled up numerous touchdowns. I could have been an MVP candidate! Why do I always get the raw deal?

Or I could view the final two games as an amazing blessing.

What a gift to carry the ball in a meaningful game! What an honor to perform in front of my teammates! What if I had never had this opportunity? How LUCKY was I?

The lens through which we view life is our own *choice*. I chose the positive lens.

And we all have that same choice to make in our everyday lives.

In our work lives, our satisfaction is largely driven by how we view success. Of course we want to strive for more. Of course we must be relentless in our pursuit of excellence. But we must find the balance between ambition and perspective.

Are we fixated on the clients we lose or grateful for the clients we have? Do we focus on the thousands of rejections we receive in the sales process or celebrate the times we break through? Do we give up if we get passed over for a promotion or double down on our effort to prove our true worth? Do we focus on our defeats or treasure our wins?

If we search for the negative, we will find it.

But if we *choose* to focus on the positive, we can keep fighting for greatness!

The same is true in our personal lives. Do we obsess over the relationships that drive us crazy? Or do we appreciate the incredible love of the solid relationships in our lives? Do we spiral into a black hole over our mounting financial obligations? Or do we celebrate the small victories that deliver income? Do we focus on the flaws of our spouse? Or are we grateful we found someone who will tolerate *our own* foibles and shortcomings?

Our happiness is largely dictated by the lens through which we view our lives.

Staying positive is a choice. But let's not kid ourselves. It's a **difficult** choice!

Getting rejected can be *humbling.* Losing clients can be *devastating.* Platooning in our career can be *demeaning.* Financial uncertainty can be *gut-wrenching.* Relationships can be *complicated.* Marriage can be a *battle.*

Things aren't always going to go our way. Nobody goes through life without scars. We are all going to face adversity at some point in our lives. But we can't allow those losses to sap our motivation.

It's okay to get knocked on our heels every now and then. That's life. If we aren't getting hurt, we probably aren't trying hard enough.

We shouldn't try to bubble-wrap our world! We must view these setbacks as *temporary.* We must see the *possibility* of better times ahead. We have too much talent to throw in the towel and settle for a fate below our potential.

Our resilience is fueled by our mindset. Without a positive outlook, we don't stand a chance. Why? Because the difficulties we face are real and emotional. They can overwhelm our senses and test our resolve and strength. Setbacks are a *worthy* adversary. And negativity can be an empty security blanket to deal with the pain.

To win, we must actively fight back!

If we can muster the strength to focus on the positive in the middle of a storm, we can overcome even the most difficult setback.

And we all have that ability. Everyone has the potential to be *resilient.* It all comes down to perspective.

Every rose has its thorn. But never forget that *every thorn has its rose*!

SIGN, SIGN, EVERYWHERE A SIGN!

"The universe is always speaking to us . . . sending us little messages."
—Nancy Thayer

My sister and her husband own a lake house in Southern Maine which provides the ultimate "unplugged" experience. Pontoon boats for relaxation. High-speed tubing for the adventurous. Kayaks and paddleboards for everyone. It is the type of place where troubles go to die.

One recent trip, my daughter Riley asked me to go on an early morning kayak trip around the lake. Having recently suffered some minor personal and professional setbacks, my resilience was running low. I wasn't feeling particularly motivated for the trip, but I recognized the importance of the moment. When your teenage daughter actually *asks* to spend time with you, the answer *has to be yes*!

As soon as we embarked on the trip, I knew it would be a special adventure. The sky was a brilliant azure blue. The water was clear and inviting. And the serenity and silence of the lake washed over both of us.

This particular lake was littered with hundreds of tiny islands. Five minutes into the paddle, we stumbled upon a particularly small one and decided to explore. We pulled the kayaks up on shore and surveyed the landscape. The island was less than twenty yards long. Tall pine trees formed a ring around the exterior, leaving a small patch of grass and sand in the center. Were we the first ones to discover this slice of paradise?

We excitedly pushed on toward the clearing. As we burst through the trees, I looked down and stopped in my tracks. *A bolt of lightning. Saul of Tarsus getting knocked off the horse. A* ***sign*** *from the universe!*

Resting peacefully in the sand was a flat, polished rock that was artistically decorated and adorned with the following message: ***Stars Can't Shine Without Darkness.***

Was someone expecting me? Did someone know I would be in that exact spot at that exact moment? Did someone know I *needed* to see this?

It was a sign. It was instant perspective. *Adversity presents opportunities.*

And don't we all occasionally need a sign to help guide us in our own lives?

Slogans can't replace effort. Signs can't replace desire and appreciation. Surrounding ourselves with posters and bumper stickers won't change the trajectory of our lives on their own. In order to recover from our setbacks, we need more than platitudes and trite sayings. But when it comes to powering through our most difficult moments, we need all the help we can get! Why ignore the universe? Why dismiss a potential boost to our confidence?

Resilience is a mindset. If we want to push forward, we can't close ourselves off to the world. We can't do it by ourselves. We need to be in "receive mode" for help.

Sometimes, help might come from a friend or colleague.

Sometimes, help might come from a parent or child. Sometimes, help might come from a stranger demonstrating particular empathy in the moment.

Sometimes, help might come from a preternatural rock in the middle of an uninhabited island!

In dark times, even the slightest sliver of hope can keep us moving in the right direction. A large deal on the horizon. A new client with major potential. A student who is starting to turn the corner. A player who finally *listens.* A child who makes strides toward reaching his or her potential. An icy relationship that shows progress toward thawing out.

But in order to keep that hope alive we have to *believe* the future holds promise. If we believe we can't win, we will lose. If we believe the world is stacked against us, we will be alone. If we believe all hope is lost, there is only room for despondence and lethargy.

Why close ourselves off to the *possibility* of a better future?

Sometimes we need little reminders. Sometimes we need a sign from the universe that everything is going to be okay.

Sometimes, a rock is a rock. Sometimes, it is a personal message to keep *fighting.*

We all deserve happiness. We all deserve a better future. We all deserve the opportunity to *shine in the darkness.*

We need to stay resilient. *The signs are all around us.*

BLOCKCHAIN, BITCOIN, "DILLY DILLY!" AND OTHER THINGS I *PRETEND* TO UNDERSTAND

"Vulnerability is often seen as a weakness; it's actually a sign of strength!"
—Patrick Leoncini

Have you ever spoken confidently about something you know little about?

There I was in the middle of a serious client meeting when the dreaded "blockchain" topic reared its ugly head. Like most people, I have heard of blockchain and know enough to be dangerous. But to me, it is like dealing with the sun. Don't stare directly at it. Just get a sense of it.

"What do know about blockchain?" my client asked.

"Plenty," I lied. "It's a virtual ledger for cryptocurrency and it's *very* powerful."

This seemed to satisfy the client. Although the reality is, I don't *really* know what cryptocurrency is (Bitcoin? Of course!) and I'm not even sure if I could define a "ledger."

Feeling a little insecure, I quickly turned the conversation around.

"I'd love to know more about *your* blockchain strategy!"

For the next thirty minutes, the client waxed poetically about his grand design. Apparently, blockchain was creating a paradigm shift. They were smashing silos. New markets were emerging. *Blah, blah.*

At the end of the discussion, my colleague and I walked out very confident.

"That was a *great* meeting!"

"Dilly Dilly!" I screamed with enthusiasm.

We both laughed and shook hands.

But it really wasn't a great meeting. I wasted the client's time by making him answer a question I couldn't possibly understand. And I wasted my time by having to listen. What purpose did that serve?

And to add insult to injury, I don't really even know what "Dilly Dilly" means!

Why was I so afraid to admit a vulnerability? And why do we feel the need to bury our heads in the sand and cover up those blind spots in our work and personal lives?

In our work lives, there is always going to be an issue we don't fully understand. We can't expect to be the expert in *everything.* That is why we have teammates. That is why we have specialists. We can't and shouldn't have to do it alone.

Even the most seasoned salesperson gets flustered. Even the most tenured professor gets stumped. Even the most decorated coach gets confused. Even the best student gets stymied. Even the most senior attorney gets caught off guard. It's okay. We are not machines.

But we have to own it!

There is nothing wrong with saying "I don't really know, but I'll find out!" It demonstrates a refreshing honesty *and* it opens the possibility of learning new things. If we are constantly masking our shortcomings, how can we grow? How can gain proper perspective?

And we might even find that by displaying the naked truth, the person sitting across from us will admit they really don't understand the concept either.

Imagine if we all got real with one another? Imagine how much more we could accomplish! Imagine how much more trust we could earn. The "smartest" person in the room isn't always the smartest person in the room. We need to have faith in our instincts. And stay honest even in times of doubt.

This is even more critical in our personal lives. We all have vulnerabilities. Eventually, they will be exposed. So why try to hide them?

It's okay if you don't know how to fix that leaky faucet. Don't provide a Band-Aid fix to prove you are in control. That will only cause a flood down the road. Don't worry if you aren't good with numbers. You can't pretend the bills are adding up. That will only cause a financial tsunami in the end. And don't try to hold back those tears in *The Notebook*. Nobody is going to think less of you if you let it all out (well, maybe a *little* less).

But the point is, it does us no good to pretend. We are who we are. Honesty and transparency should be valued in any relationship. Ignoring our blind spots only stifles our growth and causes larger issues down the road.

The more we "keep it real" in the good times, the better off we will be when the tide turns against us. *Resilience* requires us to deal with the raw truth. We must recognize that we are in a tough jam. We must accept accountability for our predicament. And we must demonstrate confidence by taking definitive action to come back stronger than ever.

We can all do it. But it starts with owning up to our blind spots and making appropriate choices. This allows us to maintain a proper perspective. Burying our heads in the sand and glossing over our weak points will only delay our pain.

We can't understand blockchain unless we dig in. We can't get rich on Bitcoin unless we study the economic fundamentals. We can't learn how to fix things unless we watch some YouTube videos and make the effort. We can't learn how to love unless we are willing to be vulnerable and get hurt.

We can't grow unless we admit our weaknesses and actively work to improve.

The choice is ours. Let's all toast to **keeping it real** from here on out.

Dilly Dilly!

LIFE LESSONS FROM FRANKIE THE FORKLIFT GUY

"You never know when a moment, or a few sincere words, can have an impact on a life."
—Zig Ziglar

I knew him as Frankie the Forklift Guy. He was a tornado of energy and a frenzied worker. I have no idea where he is today. But he taught me more about resilience and empathy than anyone I have ever known.

Many years ago, I was struggling to make it as a screenwriter in Hollywood. My projects were tanking, my savings were dwindling, and my resilience was wearing thin. I didn't have much time left to make it in the Dream Factory.

Fortunately, a good friend, Tom Reyes, was gracious enough to arrange a temporary job working in his beverage warehouse at Harbor Distributing. It provided just enough income to extend my dream. After a life of white-collar jobs, my blue-collar education was about to begin!

I was assigned to the "breakage" room. Here, my responsibilities included such glamourous tasks as picking through broken shards of glass, washing the bottles, and wielding a smoking hot glue gun to secure new twelve-pack containers. Now *that* was *maximizing* my college education!

At this point in my life, many of my goals were falling by the wayside. I was toiling in the bowels of a warehouse and about as far away from the Oscar podium as one could imagine. But I hunkered down, worked hard and traded in my dream of stardom for my dream of rising above my current position. Baby steps back to the top!

After a few months, I finally got my big "break." No more sliced fingers and scalding burns. I was called out of the breakage room into the brave ranks of the forklift fraternity!

In the hierarchy of the warehouse, the forklift operators are at the top of the pyramid. And among those chosen few, no one was more respected than Frankie. He was fast. He was efficient. And he rarely took a break when he was on the clock. If something needed to get done, all eyes turned to Frankie.

On my first assignment, Frankie and I were responsible for moving two pallets of beer from one side of the warehouse to the other. I deftly maneuvered the giant tongs into place, lifted the wooden pallet, and sailed across the warehouse with pride. If I could do this, I could do anything!

But suddenly, I hit a bump. *Crash! Pop! Boom!* Twenty-four cases of beer were now splayed across the concrete floor. *The horror!*

The depth of my despair was exponentially magnified in that moment. My confidence crashed along with the beer as the negative thoughts flowed: *I had let my wife, Jennifer, down by leading her on a wild goose chase out West. I had let my parents down by wasting my college education. I had let myself down by not maximizing my talent. I had let my friend down by ruining his merchandise. Was I destined for a life in the breakage room?*

Just then I felt a hand on my shoulder. It was Frankie.

"Happens all the time, buddy," he beamed. "Don't sweat it. We've been meaning to get that bump fixed."

In less than two minutes, he helped me clean up the entire mess and sent the rest of the bottles back to breakage for repacking. Life in the warehouse did not miss a beat, and the "incident" did not even get a mention on lunch break. Hope and optimism quickly replaced abject despair.

Frankie taught me ***two valuable lessons*** in that moment that can fuel resilience in all of us:

1) Things are rarely as bad as they seem in the moment.

Accidents happen all the time and people make mistakes. In difficult times, we become our own worst critics as negative thoughts quickly cascade into despair. We need to rise above the desperation in the moment and strive for much-needed perspective.

In my case, I still had talent and a bright future ahead of me. My wife and parents still supported me, and no amount of broken glass was going to shatter that bond. My friend was not going to lose his business over a few broken bottles. It was a simple miscue and not a harbinger of disastrous things to come.

But would I ever have achieved that *perspective* without a simple act of *empathy*?

2) Empathy is a *powerful* choice.

Everyone faces some type of challenge. Perhaps a crisis in confidence. Perhaps an unsettled home life. Perhaps a recent mistake or tough loss. At some point, everyone reaches a breaking point. But the smallest act of compassion can have a major impact on someone's life.

Frankie had a choice. He could have whirled right past me and gone about his business. He certainly didn't know I was near a breaking point in my life, and he didn't need to offer support and consoling words. But his simple act of empathy changed my perspective forever.

We all face setbacks at some point in our lives.

But we all have the ability to recover. We all have the ability to come back stronger than ever. We all have the ability to accomplish our dreams.

We simply need to maintain our perspective in difficult times and keep moving forward.

And we need to realize that a little empathy can go a long way in our lives and the lives of all those we touch.

Just ask Frankie the Forklift Guy. A simple, kind act can make this world a better place.

THE DANGER OF MAJORING IN THE MINORS

"Greatness and nearsightedness are incompatible. Meaningful achievement depends on lifting one's sights and pushing toward the horizon."
—Daniel Pink

The pace of modern life has accelerated to breakneck speeds in the digital era. With the proliferation of technology, we are always tuned in, always accessible, and always accountable in our work lives. In addition, with an increasing number of dual income households, our home life has become a high-wire juggling act of children's activities and social events. There is nothing inherently wrong with this as we want the best for ourselves and for our family. But with all the noise and constant demands on our time, it can become difficult to maintain perspective. It is easy to get so wrapped up in the whirlwind of competition and comparisons that we lose sight of the big picture.

Every now and then, we have to step back and take a deep breath. Are we working to satisfy our own ego or to make a better life for our family? Are we more concerned about what other people think of us than what we think of ourselves? Do we worry more about our children winning a contest than we do about their development? In short, are we properly focused on the truly important things in our lives?

There is a danger of "majoring in the minors." In business, we often start off with the lofty goals of solving our customer's problems or advancing the progress of mankind. But we too often slip to focus on the minor goals of winning an award or impressing our colleagues. In our family lives, we start off with the major goals of instilling our children with moral values and raising them to maximize their potential. But it is easy to slip into the minor focus of winning a competition or acing a standardized test. We want to maintain strong, lasting friendships and build a foundation of trust. But too often we focus on the shortcomings of others and unleash judgment instead of compassion.

We need to focus on the majors. If we relentlessly help our customers solve their problems, the minor outcome of awards and accolades will follow. If we build a foundation of confidence and resilience in our children, they will succeed in any area of life. If we focus on trust and forgiveness in our friendships, we won't be shackled with the negative energy of jealousy and judgment in our relationships. Life is too short to be swept up in the minutiae swirling about us every day. Focusing on the major things in our life is both healthy and uplifting. We need to rise above the noise and be that shining example of hope in this world.

The minor outcomes and circumstances are not necessarily negative things. I am not suggesting that we renounce our worldly goods and move to the desert. Financial success can be liberating. There is nothing wrong with owning a big house (sign me up!) or a fancy boat (sign up a friend!). There is nothing wrong with urging our child to excel in competition or wanting our son or daughter to attend an Ivy League school. Who doesn't want the best life possible for our family? Dream big!

But those outcomes should not be our main focus. We need to keep providing value for our clients. We need to keep loving and supporting our family. We need to keep building relationships based on trust and respect. We cannot go wrong by focusing on the major goals in our life. It's all about the bigger picture. The minor things will take care of themselves.

It will not be easy. The distractions and societal pressures will be everywhere. We will be constantly tempted to focus on minor outcomes and perceptions. Stay strong! Stay resilient! Focus on the horizon! We need to maintain our health and our positive outlook. If we do, we are destined to have a *major* impact on this world.

WHAT'S DONE IS DONE

"Close the door on the past. You don't try to forget your mistakes, but you can't dwell on them."
—Johnny Cash

William Shakespeare (perhaps unwittingly) offers one of the most powerful messages for everyday resilience. In Act 3, Scene 2 of *Macbeth*, Lady Macbeth implores her husband: "Things without all remedy should be without regard: what's done, is done." Granted, it seems a little too callous and nonchalant in the context of the premeditated murder of King Duncan. But that little detail aside, this sentiment remains a key aspect of everyday resilience in our work and personal lives.

In our work lives, we tend to look back and analyze every mistake and wrong decision. What if I had presented the client with a better option? What if I had performed to my potential? What if I had stayed at that job until the company went public? What if I had taken a chance on a hot start-up instead of marching down the conventional path? What if I had studied harder? What if I had made that save or completed that pass?

Regret is a natural by-product of failure, but we cannot allow it to paralyze us. We are where we are because of our decisions and actions. But our future is not dictated by our past. *What's done is done!* Regardless of our situation, we need to move forward with confidence. It's never too late to start all over again. It's never too late to rededicate ourselves to the task at hand. It's never too late to become the success we always knew we could be.

The same is true in our personal lives. What if I had stayed in a committed relationship? What if I had taken that piece of good advice? What if I had started my nest egg sooner? What if I had been stricter with my children? What if I hadn't taken my friends for granted? We can't dwell on our regrets. We can't un-ring the bell. Living in the past is never the answer. *What's done is done!* We need to keep our eyes forward and not on the rearview mirror. There is nothing we have done in the past that can't be forgiven. There is nothing we have done in the past that negatively defines our future. Nothing we have done prevents us from achieving ultimate happiness and satisfaction.

But that outlook is harder to discern when we are in the middle of a crisis or setback. In these difficult moments, it seems as though the world has turned against us. Loneliness and despair creep in and nest. We must be the only ones who have experienced failure! We must be the only ones who have suffered a loss! *Nonsense.* If we are to stay resilient, we must realize that we are not alone. If we are to stay resilient, we must realize that it is okay to stumble as long as we keep moving forward.

No one is immune from the slings and arrows of outrageous misfortune. (Another tip of the cap to the Bard of Avon!) It will not be easy. It will not happen overnight. But we will recover with grace. Resilience is a mindset, and it starts with the realization that we cannot change the past. *What's done is done!*

WHERE ARE YOU ON THE PATH?

"Comparison is the thief of joy!"
—Franklin Delano Roosevelt

The beach in Santa Monica, California, is, in my opinion, one of the most beautiful places in the world. With sweeping views of the Pacific Ocean punctuated by the craggy expanse of the Santa Monica Mountains, Santa Monica never disappoints. Many years ago, my wife and I lived in a tiny apartment right on that beach with a sliver view of the ocean. It was glorious. One morning, I went out for my customary jog along the main strand winding through the California coastal beach towns. A few miles into the run, an older man raced past me. A couple minutes earlier, I was at peace with myself, soaking in the sunshine and the gorgeous views. Now, I was discouraged by this old man's pace and felt inferior and subordinate. Was I really getting *dusted* by this guy? As if he could read my mind, the old man whirled around and ran back toward me.

"How far are you into the run?" he asked earnestly.

"Three miles or so," I shot back.

"I just started," the old man huffed. "I hope I can move at *half* your pace when I am three miles in!"

And then it hit me. Why was I so focused on the progress of someone else? Why was I letting him dictate my happiness? Everyone joins the path at different points in the journey. And we never know what is going on in someone else's world. Why couldn't I focus on my own journey and be happy giving my best effort on the run? And, in similar fashion, why do many of us take this same approach in our work and personal lives?

For younger employees entering the workforce, it appears their older colleagues have a significant advantage. This can be frustrating. *Why do the seasoned veterans get all the good accounts? Why can't I be as confident in a business setting? When will people take me seriously?* They want to fast-forward their lives in order to gain valuable experience as well as additional clout and money. Understandable. Conversely, the older employees can view their younger counterparts as a threat to their livelihood. *How can I ever learn this new technology in order to keep up? How can I maintain my energy to compete with these young guns? How can I stay relevant in this rapidly changing world?*

The reality is that all workers are on a different point on the path. And all of us have our own strengths and weaknesses. If we are just starting out, we have raw energy as an asset, and our older colleagues can teach us so much about the business. If we are a seasoned veteran, we have experience and confidence on our side, and our younger colleagues can help us adapt to a new culture or master a new technology. Regardless, we all have *so much* we bring to the table. We cannot waste our time with jealousy or self-critical introspection about our progress. We need to set our own pace and keep driving down the path. Only we know where we are in the journey.

The same is true in our personal lives. We may get married early and settle into a big home with our family. Or it may take us longer to find the right person and settle down. We may have a tougher time making friends or we could have a massive social circle. And all that could change instantly at any point in the journey. We cannot compare ourselves with others whom we perceive to have so much more. We don't know where they are on their path. We don't know what makes them happy. And we shouldn't focus there. We need to focus on our own journey. At some point we will share the path with others who could be moving faster. We can't let their apparent success influence *our own* vision of success and happiness.

This is especially true when we suffer a setback. Losing a job. Losing a game. Ending a relationship. During these times, it can seem that everyone else is blissfully zooming by us on the path. Why can't we get a break? But the reality is that most people have some challenge in their lives. If we are going to be resilient and move forward (and I *know* we are!), we can't let others dictate our happiness. We need to focus on our *own* next steps. We need to be action-oriented and move our *own* lives forward. We need to stay positively focused on our *own* happiness. There are oceans and mountains and beautiful vistas all around us. It's time to get rolling!

Let's stick to our own pace. Work hard but take time to enjoy the views. Focus on our own peace and happiness. Just when we think we are nearing the end of the path, another one will pop up with fresh and fascinating twists and turns. And when the path leads to a dark tunnel, we must keep moving forward until we break into the bright sunlight! Our journey is never complete. And our path will never end.

DON'T WAIT FOR SASAKI'S PHONE BOOTH

"Time and tide wait for no man."
—Geoffrey Chaucer

High atop a grassy hill in Otsuchi, Japan, overlooking the Pacific Ocean, sits an antique white phone booth. Inside, there is a single, archaic rotary phone with a small notepad and pen. It is jarringly out of place in this rural setting. Yet the impact of this vintage landmark is beyond description.

The phone booth's owner, Itaru Sasaki, purchased the kiosk in 2010 to help him deal with the loss of his beloved cousin. The phone booth was both a symbolic gesture and a practical way to "call" his cousin and tell him how much he loved and missed him. He soon dubbed it the "Wind Phone" as his voice would be carried from the booth out onto the winds to connect with the afterlife.

If that were the end of the story, it would be a unique and interesting piece.

But less than a year later, on March 11, 2011, a massive 9.1 magnitude earthquake struck Eastern Japan. The subsequent tsunami sent black waves of devastation across the peninsulas and fishing villages along the coast.

In a single day, nearly 16,000 Japanese lost their lives. The small town of Otsuchi was particularly decimated. The entire province was underwater, and over 10 percent of the population was wiped out within hours.

The normally stoic and proud people of Otsuchi now had to deal with grief on an impossible scale. So where did they turn? They turned to Sasaki's idyllic phone booth.

At first, only a few villagers ventured up the hill to share their grief in the phone booth. But soon, word spread across the entire eastern province about the cathartic powers of the "Wind Phone." After a few months, Sasaki's property resembled a Japanese *Field of Dreams*. Thousands of people embarked on a pilgrimage to the site to check in with their deceased loved ones and express their continued love.

To date, over 10,000 Japanese survivors have entered Sasaki's phone booth. A microphone was installed as part of a documentary, and the subsequent film, as well as the podcast from "This American Life," depicts the poignant and heart-wrenching "conversations" with the dead.

It is incredibly powerful.

But while the story demonstrates the beauty and reverence of how we grieve, there is another subtext and message for those left behind.

Why wait for the "Wind Phone" to communicate our appreciation and gratitude?

In our work lives, there are countless people who make our success possible. Our coworkers who inspire us with their work ethic. Our admin and support staff who simplify our lives daily. Our boss who removes obstacles and helps us safely navigate the internal waters. How often do we express our gratitude? How often do we tell them how much we appreciate their support?

And what about our clients? They have placed their trust in us. They have decided to embrace our brand, heed our advice, or benefit from our products. How often do we thank them for their business? How often do we pledge our loyalty in return?

Circumstances change quickly. Clients, coworkers and staff are in constant flux. We never know how much time we have in our current situation. Why not take the time to express our gratitude *today*?

The same is true in our personal lives. Our parents have sacrificed so much for us to live a better life. If you have had a chance to say a long goodbye, you are blessed. If they are still alive, why wait for the phone booth?

Our spouse or significant other takes on so much so we can be happy. How often do we express our true appreciation for their support and contributions?

Our children are dealing with tough decisions and pressure as they mature into adulthood. Do we tell them how incredibly proud we are even when they fail?

And what about the coach who stood in the rain trying to make us better? Or the teacher who stayed late to help the night before a test? Or the athlete who never complained about playing time but still practiced hard for the team? Or the classmate who helped us understand the homework? Or the friend who always listened in our time of need?

Don't they deserve to know how much we care?

It is so easy to take those closest to us for granted. Sometimes, we need to step back and appreciate all the amazing people in our lives. Sasaki's phone booth provides the ultimate perspective.

Not all of us can easily express our emotions. It is hard for some of us to share. That is okay. I am not suggesting that we need to run around hugging each other and singing "Kumbaya." Everyone has their own way of showing gratitude. A knowing wink or a sincere nod can be an understated but powerful expression.

But we are *all* capable of *some* acknowledgement. We are all capable of expressing appreciation and gratitude. We are all capable of letting our inner circle know how much we appreciate them.

Tell those closest to you how much you care. Do it today.

Don't wait for Sasaki's phone booth.

THE GUY NEXT TO YOU AT THE DRIVING RANGE DOESN'T CARE ABOUT YOUR AWFUL SLICE

"Success finally came my way when I got over the feeling that I didn't belong."
—Steve Buscemi

Believe it or not, when I first picked up golf in my late twenties, I was even worse than I am now (Didn't think that was possible, eh?). Every time I made it to the driving range, I couldn't help but think that everyone was staring at me. I would hit terrible shot after terrible shot, feeling I was the only one *not* smashing the ball 300 yards down the middle. It got so bad that eventually I would only practice when I was sure no one else was around. I just didn't belong with all those other great golfers.

One morning, I was struggling through my solitary routine, when three other golfers appeared out of nowhere. I felt claustrophobic and tense and immediately started hitting the worst shots of my life (and that is saying something!). I was certain they were chronicling my every misfire and would have some good laughs at my expense later that day.

After a complete whiff, I prepared to pack up my clubs and slink off the range. But as I put my bag over my shoulder, I noticed the guy next to me shank a ball into the woods. Then the guy next to him dribbled the ball a few feet off the tee. Another guy had his earphones on and was swinging away in his own world. Nobody was focused on what *I* was doing. Nobody was judging me for my failures. Every one of them either had their own issues or were so caught up in their own routines, they weren't interested in mine. Yet I had launched into self-imposed isolation and nearly quit the game entirely because I *perceived* I was the only one who didn't belong. I *perceived* that other people were judging, watching, and staring at my failures. The *reality* could not have been further from the truth!

How many times have we done this in our own lives? At the office, we may be new or simply not as confident in our subject matter. Everyone else seems to be an expert. We don't speak up in meetings for fear of being ridiculed. We fail to share our original ideas because we sense others on the team have already thought of them. We work in isolation so others won't see our mistakes. We constantly feel as though we are behind and unable to learn the material as fast as everyone else.

In our personal lives, we feel as though everyone else has it all figured out. We *must* be the only ones in financial trouble. We *must* be the only ones with children who struggle in the classroom. We *must* be the only ones without a big house or a brand-new car. We are afraid to dress a certain way or express our individualism because we think others might be judging us. As a result, we desperately strive to fit in. And we make decisions based on how we perceive others will react. This can have a devastating effect as we constantly try to one-up each other. Not exactly the recipe for a resilient life!

The reality is that *nobody* has it all figured out. The most confident and competent person we know has their moments of doubt and weakness. People on the team are not focused on our mistakes and inadequacies because they are too concerned with their own. Most people run into some kind of financial trouble or legal struggle at some point in their journey. Not everyone's child gets into Harvard or Yale. None of us have the "perfect" life.

We will all struggle at some point. We will all make mistakes. But if we stifle our creative ideas and stop expressing our unique qualities, that is not okay. If our lifestyle and actions are based on how others will perceive us, that is not okay. If we are afraid to fail and stop taking risks because of what others think, that is not okay. If we are going to live a resilient life, we must constantly move forward with the conviction that we are making the right choices for *us*. Not the right choices for someone else.

There is nothing holding us back from greatness. We don't need someone else's approval to accomplish our goals and dreams. This is our life. And we belong. So speak up in those meetings! Share your crazy ideas! Wear your skinny jeans or your Chubbies with pride! Never apologize for your passion! Don't be afraid to fail in a spectacular fashion! Swing as hard as you can on the driving range and don't worry about the potential judgment from all sides. The person next to you doesn't have it figured out either.

A DIFFERENT KIND OF HERO

"I don't want to change the world. I just want to make my corner a little better."
—Aaron Burdett

What would the world be like without our heroes? Perhaps our hero is a professional athlete or a decorated Olympian. Perhaps a movie star or a musical legend. Perhaps even a major titan of industry or a dynamic political figure. When we think of our heroes, we tend to think on a grand scale. We place these transformational figures in the forefront of our consciousness as they inspire us, give us hope, and pull us along to share in their triumph. Our heroes are a great source of inspiration. If they can achieve such incredible feats, perhaps so can we!

It is so important to have these lofty goals and grandiose dreams. Go big or go home! But we need to be careful how we measure our level of success. So many of us get discouraged because we don't think we are making a true difference in this world. We want to be heroes but don't understand how to get there. We dream of working in the corner office, but the CEO doesn't even know our name. We dream of winning the landmark case but get stuck with the tedious research. We dream of reaching millions of people with our message but only have a handful of subscribers.

It is easier to take our foot off the gas pedal and settle for mediocrity when our goals and dreams seem so unattainable. How can we stay resilient and constantly move forward when the finish line is such a faint dot on the horizon? We need perspective. It takes a series of smaller steps to get there. If we mentor and help the members of our immediate team, eventually our boss will take notice. If we execute the basic blocking and tackling of research and cold-calling, eventually our clients will take notice. If we take a stand and write from the heart, eventually we will build a loyal following.

Life is not a zero-sum game. We can measure our success and work toward our lofty goals by building on our smaller victories. It won't come all at once. We must be patient and continue to move forward. But we can't be a hero until we positively influence one person. When we do, we have taken a major step toward success. And then there will be no stopping us on our way to the top!

There is nothing wrong with thinking globally about our contributions to the world. Train hard for the Olympics. Dream of serving our country overseas. Find a cure for cancer. We can't ever let our dreams slip away. But understand that our journey to success happens locally.

Think about the people who have delivered joy to our lives. The teacher who patiently worked with us until we understood the concept. Or the coach who believed in us when nobody else thought we could do it. Or the family member who showed compassion in our time of need. Or the person who gave us our first job and mentored us through our transition into the "real world." These are the people who have made our lives so much richer. Aren't they changing the world by delivering a little bit of happiness? Aren't they heroes in their own right?

We need to return the favor by making our little corner of the world a better place. We don't have to be on the cover of *Sports Illustrated* to be a hero. We don't have to sell out stadiums or perform in front of global dignitaries to be a hero. We can be a hero to our children and spouse. We can be a hero to our parents. We can be a hero to our coworkers and help them achieve their goals.

We need to take pride in doing the little things right. First, we need to take care of our little corner of the world. Then we can take of the rest.

Everyone has the ability to change the world. We need to take action and work hard to make it happen. But that change happens one person and one relationship at a time. If we are a positive source of inspiration to all those around us, that is all it takes to be a hero!

WHEN THE SPOTLIGHT DIMS

"If you light a lamp for somebody, it will also brighten your path."
—Ancient Proverb

We live in an uber-connected world of twenty-four-hour news coverage, endless talk show analysis, and instantaneous access to events from around the globe. In the glare of the public spotlight, everyone from our professional athletes to our politicians to our movie stars has their slightest movements dissected and scrutinized in a perpetual media frenzy. This comes with the territory for our public figures.

Those covering these public figures scramble to create a sound bite or find that perfect catchphrase to bask in their own fifteen minutes of fame. And with the rapid proliferation of social media, we now *all* have the potential to be a "star." Snap a selfie with Pope Francis and post it on Instagram! Land a movie deal from your latest YouTube video! How many "likes" can you get on Facebook and how many "retweets" can you garner on Twitter? The world is revolving around *us* as we search for an audience to validate our star power!

I don't want to suggest that social media is the root of all evil. Quite the opposite. It has so many useful and life-changing applications that make our world a smaller place. But if we are not careful, this can create a perception that we must constantly be at the center of the universe.

As managers, since we must be the stars, it becomes tempting to take credit for the work of our team and promote ourselves over the success of the project. As teachers and coaches, it becomes tempting to only work with the best athletes or students since that will give us the most exposure to public accolades. As parents, we run the risk of leveraging our child's athletic or academic excellence to increase *our* status and recognition in the community. When the spotlight never stops shining, all perspective is lost.

If we are to maintain any sense of balance in our lives, we must realize that it is not all about us! The most effective managers defer credit to their team and work in the background to quietly remove barriers and create an atmosphere of growth. The teachers who change lives are the ones who faithfully make themselves available outside of class to inspire the student who has lost his or her way. The coaches who become legends work before and after practice with the athletes who have given up on themselves. And the well-adjusted parents recognize the importance of working selflessly with their children and remaining humble in the face of their child's own success.

Our greatest accomplishments will not be performed in front of a massive audience. Our most satisfying work will not receive a national award. Our legacy may not play out in a Hall of Fame induction ceremony. But away from the spotlight, we will know that we changed the world by following our passion and making at least one person better.

If we are constantly playing to an audience and preoccupied with how others perceive us, we cannot achieve our own goals. In fact, we won't even recognize our own goals! Eventually, no matter how successful we think we are, we will hit a setback in the journey. During this time, the spotlight will dim and we will feel all alone. If we have lived our life seeking attention and making it all about us, this period can be especially desolate and devastating. But if we have given support to others, been a mentor to others and put our team's needs above our own, we will bounce back with ease. After all, by helping others become the stars, we have built a loyal support network that will catapult us back to success. In this moment, we will find our true character. In this moment, we will find our resilience. In this most difficult moment, we will now feel like the star of the show!

We need to help others achieve their goals, and we cannot lose sight of our own. And never forget, the true stars shine when the spotlight dims.

FOCUS ON THE TASK AT HAND

"Concentrate all your thoughts upon the work at hand. The sun's rays do not burn until brought into focus."
—Alexander Graham Bell

For some of us, reciting the Latin language may conjure up painful memories of "pluperfect" tenses that hearken back to those awkward high school years. But despite the negative connotations that could propel us into *rigor mortis,* Latin has provided us with the foundation for our English language and some of the simplest yet most profound mottos in modern American life. *Carpe diem. E. Pluribus Unum. Semper Fidelis!*

But St. Ignatius Loyola, the founder of the Jesuit Order, offered advice with the most powerful Latin phrase for everyday resilience: ***Age Quod Agis***. Literally translated, it means "Do what you are doing." But, practically, it is encouragement to keep going and focus on the task at hand. In this hectic, turbo-charged modern world, it is easy to become distracted, frustrated and confused by the many roles we play in our life. Focusing on the task at hand can help us stay balanced and ensure we do not become overwhelmed by our responsibilities.

When we are at work, we need to concentrate on the responsibilities we have to our boss, our clients, our students, our teammates and our company. Our thoughts and energy should be solely dedicated to advancing the cause of our organization. Our work can be incredibly gratifying and rewarding if we pour our soul into it and stay focused. But when we leave our place of employment, we need to leave thoughts of work behind. We are now a father, mother, husband, wife, son or daughter. It's time to concentrate on taking care of our family, which will lead to a much more peaceful life on the home front.

Too often we are physically located in one area of our life, but mentally focused elsewhere. How can we achieve maximum efficiency in our work life if we are constantly distracted by thoughts of financial pressure, child care duties, or marital concerns? How can we connect and care for our family when we have so many unfinished tasks and constant demands at work? It is not easy, but we must realize that when we are in the office, that is our world. When we are at home, that is our world. We can achieve so much more satisfaction in our lives if we can maintain that distinction and that concentration. *Age quod agis.*

But it is even more important to put this plan into practice when we experience a setback. The loss of a job, a tactical mistake at work or at home, the ending of a relationship or a fallout with our family can knock us on our heels. Even worse, these setbacks can lead to depression and a loss of energy that further exacerbate a negative situation. This is one of the few times in our life when it is okay to be self-focused. Take the time to identify the issue immediately and address the problem. Our family and friends are rooting for us and need us operating at full strength! Get to the heart of the problem. Realize that inaction is never the answer and keep moving forward. The chain is only as strong as its weakest link.

While our inner circle will always be there for us, they need and expect us to come back stronger than ever. And we owe it to ourselves to do it as quickly as possible. We can't dive under the covers and curl into a ball! We need to draw on our inner strength. We need to stay positive and never make excuses. Resilience starts with focusing on the task at hand and taking an ACTIVE role in changing the course of our life. We can overcome any obstacle.

We just need to ***age quod agis***!

THE DOOR IS ALWAYS OPEN

"There is no such thing as a bad day when there's a doorknob on the inside of the door."
—Commander Paul Galanti

The Virginia War Memorial is a breathtaking monument set high atop the hills of Richmond, Virginia. Throughout the site, there are inspirational quotes by famous Virginia heroes from the wars of World War II, Korea, Vietnam, and the Persian Gulf. While all the quotes are thought-provoking and emotional, one in particular, by Commander Paul Galanti, stands out above the rest.

Commander Galanti was a Skyhawk fighter pilot in Vietnam before being shot down by the enemy and captured. He remained a prisoner of war under brutal conditions for nearly seven years until his release on February 12, 1973. His quote and outlook on life, after adjusting to the real world, nearly stopped me in my tracks:

"There is no such thing as a bad day when there's a doorknob on the inside of the door."

I get the chills every time I read it. Think about the harsh punishment and abject loneliness Commander Galanti had to endure for years. Departing this horrific prison was not an option. Instead of harboring resentment and blaming others for his misfortune, he emerged from this ordeal with a new outlook on life. How could he have a bad day when freedom became a reality? He celebrated moving around freely, engaging in human dialogue, and breathing in the fresh air. Now, that is perspective!

Having a particularly tough commute to work? At least we have a car and the freedom to go wherever we want! Going through an unbearable negotiation with a difficult client? At least we have a job with the ability to find more clients. Wishing for more money at the end of each month? Who doesn't? At least we have enough to meet our basic needs. I know we all face a roller coaster each day in our career and family lives. Certainly, some days are better than others. But instead of complaining about what we don't have, let's try to channel Commander Galanti and appreciate the simple freedoms we enjoy on a daily basis.

In addition, I have seen way too many people ignore the doorknob and create their own self-imposed imprisonment. They feel trapped by their perceived weaknesses and give up on reaching their true potential. Sometimes, they would rather sit on the sidelines than pour their heart into something and risk failure. Creating excuses that justify this inaction makes failure more bearable. Don't fall into this trap! The reality is that we are much more talented than we will ever know. If no one is holding us back, why would we hold ourselves back? We need to take action! We may fail. But that bold step outside our world will give us the fresh perspective and confidence to keep moving forward.

Some people fail to see the doorknob because their profession brings a certain level of security. I recently had one friend tell me he is miserable in his job, but has to stick it out fifteen more years in order to get his pension. Fifteen years! That is a life sentence if we are not feeling fulfilled. We cannot passively sit back and wait for the moving walkway of life to deliver us to a predetermined destination. We have options. We must venture out and forge our own path to success. We must believe that we have something unique to offer the world. We must not be afraid to let our talents shine.

The doorknob is right in front of us. All we have to do is turn it and open the door into our next great adventure in life.

PARADISE IN A CVS PARKING LOT

"Find your beach."
—Corona advertising slogan

There is a "beach" bar on the Delaware shore, Bethany Boathouse, located near a Holiday Inn Express in the parking lot of a CVS. A man-made drainage ditch provides a "water view," and it sits just off the highway within earshot of traffic. Yet, miraculously, once inside it feels like paradise.

Each night, the bar offers live music and free-flowing island drinks to go with a constantly-swirling, gentle breeze. More importantly, there are good friends and family to take your mind off the neon signs and asphalt. There is no logical reason why this concept should work. *But it does.* The atmosphere and inspiration comes from the inside.

And that is a good reminder for all of us. The best things in life come from the inside. Love. Motivation. Inspiration. Resilience. It doesn't matter what is happening in the chaos all around us. We need to find our happy place. We need to find our inner Boathouse!

In our work lives, we are all grinding. Answering proposals and cold-calling under intense pressure. Preparing for client presentations in dark conference rooms. Tweaking our business plans while holed up in the office. Teaching in hot classrooms. Coaching in the rain and the humidity. It can be overwhelming at times.

It takes hard work and enormous sacrifice. On the outside, it can seem hopeless at times. But we can't just go through the motions. Every now and then we have to step back and recognize why we are grinding in the first place. *Providing security for our family. Making the world a better place. Positively influencing the next generation.* This is our live music and great friends. This will sustain us in difficult times. This is our inner motivation and our purpose.

And the same is true in our personal lives. It's not always easy on the outside. Our children can frustrate us at times. Our spouse, girlfriend or boyfriend may not appreciate our point of view. Our friends may not seem to care about our situation. Our family can generate friction and stress over the smallest matters. Sometimes, it feels as though we are battling against an aggressive riptide.

We need to relax. Our children will make mistakes, but think about all the *joy* they have given us over the years. Our significant others will disagree with us, but we will eventually find a compromise. Our friends have lives of their own, but they will always be there for us when it matters. Our family is our family. Frustrating at times, but there is no substitute! We can't let the neon glow from the CVS sign distract us. Our lives are far more beautiful when we step back with some level of perspective. We need to focus on our inner Boathouse!

But there are times when the asphalt and neon from the parking lot ruins our view. And the beach feels miles away. We all reach a breaking point. Lack of appreciation at our job. Lack of respect on the home front. Financial pressure. Health issues and illness. Major relationship woes. At times, it feels as though it will never work. How do we get back to those frozen drinks and Tom Petty cover tunes?

We can't ignore it and pretend it isn't happening. We can't stuff it all inside. We all have to deal with the realities of our everyday lives. Life is not always a beach.

But resilience is not about escape or fantasy. It's not about trite sayings and slogans. Resilience is all about perspective. Even in our darkest moments, we can't curl into a ball and give up. We can't succumb to the trials and tribulations of our everyday lives. There is always a sliver of hope. And that hope is different for everyone. If we don't see it right away, we have to keep looking!

We can find our purpose, hope, and happiness anywhere. It doesn't have to be on a fancy trip or at an expensive dinner. It doesn't have to look beautiful and perfect on the outside. It doesn't matter what the world sees. We need to find it for ourselves. The best things in life are on the inside.

And sometimes we can find paradise in a CVS parking lot.

EVERYDAY RESILIENCE PROFILE ON PERSPECTIVE: MEET "MR. GENE" LEFEGED

Ladies and gentlemen, meet the one and only Gene "Mr. Gene" Lefeged! Shot in the leg serving his country in Vietnam. Unemployed and nearly penniless after returning home. Drove a bus at a local Catholic grade school to make ends meet. Persevered and prospered at the school for forty-four years. Left an incredible legacy of kindness and compassion that influenced an entire generation of students and faculty.

Mr. Gene's life story, at face value, is a simple narrative of perseverance and loyalty. But looking deeper at the choices he made and the lives he positively impacted, Mr. Gene provides inspirational perspective and a model of everyday resilience.

Mr. Gene is the youngest of nine children and grew up in a modest but loving house in the Scotland neighborhood, in the suburbs of Washington, DC. At nineteen, he was drafted into the war and embarked overseas to serve in Vietnam. Immediately after he was deployed, Mr. Gene marched into a vicious firefight in the dense forest of the Ankhe Valley. A bullet ripped through his leg, but he still managed to make it out alive and even helped some of his fellow soldiers to safety.

As soon as he recovered from the injury, Mr. Gene was sent right back out into the teeth of combat. He was incredibly fortunate to avoid any additional injury, but the experience of feeling like a sitting duck weighed on him for the next few years. Finally, at the age of twenty-one, after dutifully serving his country, Mr. Gene was sent home to what he hoped would be a productive and prosperous life.

But there was no hero's welcome for many of the Vietnam veterans in those days. Ridiculed and belittled for his part in the war, Mr. Gene was turned down for dozens of jobs. He had spent his last nickel and was in danger of going down a dangerous path of depression and resentment. With nowhere else to turn, Mr. Gene walked two miles from the Scotland neighborhood to Mater Dei School, an idyllic Catholic grade school set back on a hill just off the main road. There he met Mr. Bob Barros, the president, headmaster and founder of the school. He asked him for a job. Mr. Barros politely turned him down.

It was another crushing blow for Mr. Gene. He trudged slowly back down the driveway toward a life of drudgery and despair. He was visibly angry and beyond frustrated. The war had not been fair. His treatment had not been fair. His life had not been fair. But as his mind raced toward negative thoughts and blame, he suddenly felt a hand on his shoulder.

"Hey, Gene!" Mr. Barros gently called out. "What exactly are you looking for?"

"I just want someone to give me respect!" Mr. Gene shot back.

Mr. Barros looked him solemnly in the eyes and lowered his voice to a whisper.

"It looks like you've been through a lot. But you have to continually earn respect. It can't be given."

There was something so simple yet so powerful about his delivery. Mr. Gene suddenly felt that huge chip lift off his shoulder, and he smiled for the first time since coming back home. Mr. Barros returned the smile.

"Can you drive a bus?" he asked

"Better than anyone!" Mr. Gene lied.

With that, Mr. Barros threw him the keys, and the legendary career of Gene Lefeged was born! Over the next forty-four years, Mr. Gene tackled every job imaginable at the school. Bus driver, chief custodian, building and grounds director, car pool monitor. More importantly, Mr. Gene interacted with the students and lent a sympathetic ear to their problems and a word of encouragement when they struggled. He always stayed positive and cautioned the students against taking themselves too seriously. They loved him. They trusted him. But it was not always easy for Mr. Gene.

Over the course of his career, he had to battle his old war injury, battle a devastating accident with a tractor, and battle a new war against alcoholism that nearly cost him his job. But Mr. Gene would not be denied. How could he? Mater Dei had given him the opportunity to thrive and earn respect in this world. Mater Dei was home. He would not let them down. He would not let the children down.

On his last day of employment, at the age of sixty-five, Mater Dei rolled out the red carpet for Mr. Gene. A brand new pickup truck waited for him in the main driveway. Forty-four years after Mr. Barros threw him the keys to the bus, the new headmaster, Mr. Ned Williams, threw him the keys to a shiny new pickup. It was a great moment for Mr. Gene, but it was the second best thing to happen to him that day. The best moment shortly followed. As he jumped in the truck, the entire student body began chanting his name in unison at the top of their lungs:

"Gene! Gene! Gene!"

A wave of emotion poured over Mr. Gene and tears streamed down his face. At that moment, he realized that through his resilience and perseverance, he had more than *earned* that respect!

What Does It Mean for Us?

Mr. Gene's journey can teach us so much about our own lives. How many of us feel we are entitled to respect and don't have to earn it? How many of us give up and move on to greener pastures when we face adversity in our work or home lives? How many of us still have that huge chip on our shoulder and blame others for our own setbacks and disappointments? How many of us listen to our mentors and remain open to change? Finally, in this day and age of corporate buyouts and forced early retirements, how many of us will have an opportunity to shed tears of joy at our retirement party?

Mr. Gene shows us the way. We control our own destiny. We must forge our own path and earn the respect of our colleagues and family members. We must persevere through those difficult moments in order to have the opportunity to leave a *lasting legacy* in this world. Mr. Gene is the happiest and most content retired person I have ever met. Such is the reward for leading a positive and resilient life.

And such will be our reward. Saddle up! Stay positive! Keep working hard! We need to keep making this world a better place! There are people who believe in us. Our greatest moments are yet to come.

PASSION

"Chase down your passion like it's the last bus of the night."
—Terri Guillemets

Photo by Brian Ridgway

NOW *THAT* IS GOOD HUSTLE!

"Good things may come to those who wait, but only things left by those who hustle."
—Abraham Lincoln

Hustle. It might be the greatest word in the English language. I am not referring to the negative use of the word associated with a fraud or scam. I am talking about the pure energy and effort often associated with sports or business. Hustle shows passion. Hustle shows resolve. Hustle shows grit. And, yes, hustle shows *resilience*!

It doesn't take talent to hustle. It has nothing to do with our natural intelligence or our God-given ability. Anyone can hustle! And hustle is where all the good stuff happens. Diving to make a tackle in football when the team is down by thirty points. Sprinting back on defense to take a charge in basketball. Sliding to save a goal in soccer. In the business world, staying late night after night to ensure the successful launch of a new product. Coming in early or staying late to help a struggling student find his or her way. Flying out on the weekend to see a client who cannot see us during normal business hours. These are pure hustle plays that are key to accomplishing the goals of the team.

But too often hustle is the trademark skill of the unsung hero. In this day and age, hustle tends to go unnoticed or unrecognized. Everyone wants to score the touchdown. But how many of us are willing to block in the trenches to pave the way to success? Everyone wants to make the big sale. But how many of us are willing to do the exhaustive research necessary to truly understand the customer's needs? In a culture where everyone wants to be the hero without putting in the effort, the team is destined to fail.

Great coaches understand that the accumulation of hustle outweighs pure talent on the path to victory. They reward and recognize those players who exude that effort and determination. In the same way, great managers understand that effort and hustle often point their teams toward success. They hire and promote employees who put the needs of the business first by hustling for the team. This builds a culture of resilience that feeds on that hustle.

Hustle alone does not always dictate success. We live in a results-oriented world, and it is very frustrating when our effort and passion are there, but the positive results are not. That frustration can quickly lead to apathy and indifference. Why hustle if we get the same results hanging out at the water cooler or sitting on the couch playing video games? Why hustle if no one appreciates our effort? But it is during these difficult moments of failure and introspection when hustle benefits us the most.

If we want to lead a resilient life, the LAST thing we need to do is stop hustling. There is no downside to pouring everything we have into achieving our goals. Eventually, our effort, our passion, and our enthusiasm will place us on a path toward success. *Eventually*, our hustle and grit will produce the recognition and results we need to lead a fulfilling and balanced life. We must continue to believe that our effort will make a difference. Hustle does not guarantee success, but lack of hustle almost certainly guarantees failure.

We cannot sit back and wait for success to come to us. We need to start building our own personal culture of hustle and passion now. And we need to keep the faith even if our efforts do not translate to immediate success. Soon our hustle will be contagious. We will inspire others to put forth the same amount of effort and enthusiasm. We will inspire others to believe their own goals are achievable. We will inspire others to lead a resilient life.

There is hustle inside all of us. We need to harness it, embrace it and let it guide us even when no one is watching. We are destined to leave a legacy of hard work and passion. Now THAT is good hustle!

GO BEYOND THE BARE MINIMUM

"Go the extra mile. Then go a thousand more. No one ever conquered life doing the bare minimum."
—Dan Waldschmidt

If we carefully examine the common traits behind any transformational leader, one constant emerges. Effort. Many leaders are blessed with natural talents such as vision, charisma, and intelligence. But talent alone is not enough to change the world. Walt Disney was an enormously gifted artist and a creative visionary. But his effort delivering newspapers as a side job led to his first big break drawing cartoons. The rest is history. Vince Lombardi had more charisma and motivational skills than any coach of his time. But without his decision to take on extra coaching work beyond his daily teaching responsibilities, he may never have become a legend. Sam Walton had an innate understanding of the customer's needs and an incredible savviness for business. But he likely would have never founded Wal-Mart if he didn't take a huge financial risk in opening a second five-and-dime store. All these men came to the table with natural talent and potential that could propel them to fame. Yet none of them would have succeeded without taking on extra work and pushing themselves above and beyond their own limits.

Most of us are not born with these incredible natural gifts and talent. We need to work even harder and balance even more in our lives if we want to walk down a path of success and happiness. We simply cannot afford to do the bare minimum. Yet in our work lives, that is the path we sometimes choose to travel. Do we strive for innovative ways to move our business forward, or do we settle for just staying afloat? Do we examine alternative methods that will help us more effectively connect with our students, or do we memorize the same lessons over and over? Do we run out of bounds near the goal line or do we dive into the end zone? Do we study twenty minutes for a test and hope to get a C, or do we hunker down, make sacrifices, and strive for that A? Do we grind to blow away our sales numbers or do we eke out 100 percent and play golf for the rest of the year? (Hmmm. Don't answer that last one!) But seriously, when has exhibiting the bare minimum translated into long-term success?

Unfortunately, this mentality can impact our personal lives as well. It becomes okay to come home and play video games rather than read a book or passionately pursue our hobby. It becomes okay to loaf in practice or slack off in exercise. It becomes okay to leave our dishes on the counter and assume someone else will clean them up. Does that sound like a fulfilling life? Doing the bare minimum is a recipe for mediocrity.

And when adversity strikes, it is even more important to go above the bare minimum. It takes extra effort and passion to bounce back from a setback. Unfortunately, most people go in the opposite direction. When things are going poorly, they give up entirely. The bare minimum would be an upgrade! These difficult moments are the times when we have to work *even harder* to get back on our feet. Resilience is not easy, but if we exhibit the energy, enthusiasm and effort during the down moments, it will carry over to all aspects of our life.

I'm not suggesting we need to be in constant "turbo" mode. Not all of us have the same drive. Not all of us have the same energy levels. Sometimes, we need a break. But we can still exhibit effort in everything we do. We can still push ourselves beyond our perceived limits. We can still passionately pursue a goal and fight to achieve success. We can all demonstrate resilience with just a little bit more effort.

Here is a little secret. We can actually live our entire life giving the bare minimum in effort. There are no laws requiring extra effort.

No one is going to force us to be passionate. But just because we can doesn't mean we should! While we can survive doing the bare minimum, we cannot improve our lives. We cannot master new skills. We cannot build meaningful relationships. We cannot become the best version of ourselves. Effort may not lead to financial success, but it will certainly lead to personal satisfaction. More importantly, it will ultimately lead to happiness.

We have so much to offer in both our work and personal lives. It just requires going above and beyond the bare minimum in all aspects of our lives. Let's make it happen!

THE DOUBLE-EDGED SWORD OF PASSION

"If we could live without passion, maybe we'd know some kind of peace. But we would be hollow. Passion is the source of our finest moments."
—Joss Whedon

There is nothing more satisfying than passionately pursuing our goals and ultimately achieving success. That passion drives us through the difficult times and allows us to blaze our own path to glory. Passion is one of the keys to leading a resilient life. There are countless examples of entrepreneurs who have willed their companies to the top through the sheer force of their passion. Can you imagine Apple succeeding without Steve Jobs driving his product team? Or Amazon thriving without the conviction of Jeff Bezos? These leaders were/are not only relentlessly focused, but also insanely passionate about their business.

The same is also true in the world of sports. The most passionate players are usually the most driven and successful. *And the most entertaining.* Jimmy Connors wasn't afraid to get emotional on his way to a fist-pumping US Open victory. Dennis Rodman wasn't the most gifted basketball player, but his hustle and passion lifted his teammates to multiple championships. And who can forget Lawrence Taylor wreaking havoc on the field "like a crazed dog"? The passion of these business leaders and sports figures drove them to incredible success in their respective fields and inspired a generation of Americans.

We all strive to harness that same type of passion in our everyday lives, but sometimes that passion can come with a downside. What happens when we launch a company with unbridled enthusiasm and it fails to take off? What happens when we fervently believe we can make a sale, and it unravels before our eyes? What happens when we passionately take the field and play with moxie, only to lose in the final moments? When we fall short of our goals, it makes it even harder to rebound from the defeat. Since failure was not an option, how do you recover when failure is the outcome? This disillusionment takes an even harder toll on the most passionate individuals. The same amazing optimism and passion that allowed for the possibility of success boomerangs quickly into despair when major cracks form in the plan. How do we pick up the pieces when our dreams (either large or small) have been shattered?

The reality is, while exuding passion and enthusiasm is a critical ingredient to a successful life, it is not a guarantee. Sometimes our passion and execution are there, but our timing is off. Sometimes our passion is there, but we get sidetracked by an unforeseen obstacle or injury. There are some things we simply cannot control. While failure is devastating in the moment, think how tragic it would be if we had never taken a shot at our dream in the first place? It is far more soul-crushing to passively *think* about a great business idea than to pursue that idea and fail. There is no tragedy in striking out swinging, only in criticizing from the stands. How can we expect to achieve happiness and success if we do not passionately pursue our goals? How will we ever reach our potential from the couch? Failure may be an option regardless. But if we live our life passively and without passion, it is a certainty.

Why not channel the same passion that elicits devastation upon failure into our next great adventure? The world embraces the bold. Our passion is contagious and will spread to all those we encounter along our journey. It is okay if we are not successful on our first attempt. There will be other companies. There will be other games. There will be other opportunities for victory. Sustained passion is undefeated. Passion always wins out in the end.

TAKE TIME TO CELEBRATE YOUR VICTORIES (BOTH LARGE AND SMALL)

"Cel-e-brate good times. Come on!"
—Kool and the Gang

For a classic reminder of how to celebrate, we need look no further than the championship games of major athletic events. The champagne-popping exuberance of the World Series champions in Major League Baseball. The confetti-crazed hugging of the college basketball champions in the NCAA Finals. The Stanley Cup–swigging euphoria of the hockey champions in the NHL Finals. The Disney World–wishing enthusiasm of the Super Bowl MVP in NFL Football. These are moments that elicit pure, unbridled joy from the newly crowned champions in their respective sports. And couldn't we all benefit from a similar celebration in our own lives?

Granted, not every victory is that dramatic and not every celebration warrants fireworks, confetti and a ticker-tape parade. But there are so many victories we experience in our lives, and it is important to take the time to recognize these accomplishments. When we work hard, put our mind to a task, and achieve our goal, we shouldn't be afraid to formally recognize it.

Obviously, life-changing events such as earning a major promotion, winning an award, or recognizing a milestone (anniversary, retirement, graduation) warrant a good, old-fashioned celebration. But what about the smaller victories on the path to our larger goals? A key meeting where we finally gain the trust of an important client. A great test score from our son or daughter who had been struggling at school.

Finishing a household task that was hanging over us for months. All these accomplishments are worthy of recognition, reflection and, yes, to some degree, celebration!

I'm not suggesting we fire up a ticker-tape parade every time we make the perfect pot of coffee. But taking time to recognize the small accomplishments in life can have a tremendously positive impact on our outlook and perspective.

Beyond outlook and attitude, this celebration is important for two additional reasons. First, setting goals and maintaining focus is critical to success. But sometimes we can lose perspective when we become overly obsessed with a goal. Pursuing a major goal is a journey with many milestones along the way. Whether we are starting our own business, managing a large client, or raising a child, the "finish line" can be murky and the definition of success is constantly shifting. If we do not take time to celebrate small victories along the way, we can become burned out and frustrated. A little self-recognition along our journey can keep us fresh and focused on our ultimate destination.

The second reason to celebrate has to do with that (now) familiar concept of everyday resilience. Celebrating those moments when something "good" happens will allow us to persevere and move forward when something "bad" happens. The feeling of accomplishment, when acknowledged, becomes a more powerful force than the feeling of failure. Capturing and celebrating that accomplishment allows us to return to that euphoric state and move forward with our lives during a time of difficulty. Those who recognize and appreciate the feeling of accomplishment are far more resilient and recover much quicker during a setback.

Life is not an easy journey. So why not take the time to celebrate the victories (both large and small!) that come along the way? Fist bump in the hallway! Scream out loud in the conference room. Take time for a massage! Go out for ice cream! It doesn't matter how we celebrate. Just do it. We will be stronger than ever when the storm clouds come in. And we will soar like an eagle to meet any challenge!

MAKE THE MOST OF YOUR MINUTES

"All we have to decide is what to do with the time that is given us."
—J. R. R. Tolkien

In my son Justin's freshman year at Georgetown Prep High School, I had a long discussion with him about his upcoming basketball game. In hindsight, it strikes me as a perfect analogy for everyday resilience in all of us.

The goal of my pep talk was to ensure that he took advantage of the minutes he played on the court:

You may play the whole game. You may only get in for a short time. Regardless, it is critical to make every single minute count! It is not just about scoring points. Hustle for every loose ball. Dive on the court. Make your teammates better. Play with passion and contagious enthusiasm. This is your chance! You may have a few turnovers and miss your first couple of jump shots. Do not waste your minutes sulking about the last possession. Turn the page, move forward and focus on the next play. Your minutes on the court are precious and they cannot be squandered away dwelling on the past.

In addition, you may not get as much playing time as you think you deserve. Those minutes on the bench STILL count. Do not ruin that time grumbling or, worse yet, questioning the coach or tearing down the players on the court. Spend that time cheering on your teammates, firing up the bench, and creating a positive atmosphere that will catapult the team to victory. Every player on the team matters. Every player can make the difference between winning and losing. Be the player who inspires victory.

In the same way, we must make every minute count in our work lives. It is not just about making the big sale, winning the big case, coaching the star athlete, or landing the big client. If that happens, be sure to celebrate! But it is the hustle and the enthusiasm that lead up to those moments that really matter. We need to build our business on a solid foundation by doing all the little things right and keeping that positive attitude. We will inspire our coworkers to achieve more than they thought possible.

Eventually, the entire team will take notice and we will establish a winning culture. But things may not always go our way. We may be passed over for a promotion or become marginalized by new leadership. The right people may not immediately recognize our talents. We cannot blame others for our situation. We must spend the time encouraging our teammates and working as hard as possible until people take notice. Eventually our moment will come. As long as we stay positive and focused, our talents will not stay hidden forever.

But even when we get our shot, things may not always go smoothly. Enthusiasm, effort, and a positive attitude will get us far in life. But we have all made mistakes. We have all miscalculated trends. We have all blown great opportunities. When adversity strikes, we cannot spend precious time dwelling on our misfortune. We can learn from our mistakes without curling up into a ball and feeling sorry for ourselves. Failure is never permanent. The best way to bounce back is through action! Work on acing your next big test. Work on mastering the next big presentation. Work on winning back the next big sale. Work on landing the next big client. Work on dominating your next business market. We will never get back the time we waste trying to change the past. Move forward with resilience! Be the person who inspires victory.

The same is true for everything we do in our lives. We only have four years of high school or college. We only have eighteen years until our children go away to school or the military. We only have a certain amount of time to leave our legacy. Be passionate! Stay enthusiastic! Continue to give maximum effort and keep that positive attitude even when things are not going our way! We never know how the game is going to play out. Sulking about the past will not improve our situation. We have the power to change the future through our actions. Remember, we only get one shot at this life. We need to make the most of our minutes!

PRIDE STILL MATTERS

"Great things are done by a series of small thing brought together."
—Vincent Van Gogh

We have all heard the expression "Wear the uniform with pride." This is most closely associated with the military and is the ultimate manifestation of representing something bigger than one person. Men and women who don the military uniform uphold the highest standards of the American people and take ownership of the incredible responsibility that comes with the uniform.

While I have never had the privilege of representing our country, I do recognize the power of taking pride in the uniform. The Marine, the pro basketball player, and the firefighter, to name a few, all put on their uniforms and go to work. The uniform allows these individuals to bond over a common mission and strive for a shared goal driven by pride.

In this pop culture of focusing on the incredible, we are trained to focus on those high-profile, heroic moments. But the Marine has to learn discipline by making up his or her bed before saving our country from terrorists. The basketball player has to shoot countless foul shots during practice before sinking the winning free throw on national television. The firefighter has to change the oil in the fire engine before rushing into a burning building to save a family. Little things matter in their everyday lives. And they must take pride in all of them.

In the same way, the salesman has to make numerous cold calls before landing the hallmark client. The lawyer has to file thousands of routine motions before winning a landmark case. The parent has to drive his or her child to endless practices before that child can achieve athletic success. People are performing smaller acts every day without fanfare or the adoration of screaming fans. And performing these tasks with pride makes them *heroic*.

But not everyone wears a "uniform," and sometimes it is not easy to take pride in our everyday routine at home or in the office. Mundane tasks can drain our motivation and cause us to produce work that does not meet our highest standards. *Filling out the spreadsheet. Cleaning the kitchen. Proofreading the proposal.* Performing these tasks does not inspire us, and it becomes one more thing to check off, rather than one more challenge to conquer and celebrate. How do we stay resilient?

As ordinary as these tasks may seem, they are still important and still something we should take pride in completing. Major accomplishments are sometimes the culmination of a series of smaller tasks. Unless those seemingly insignificant tasks are done with pride, we may never achieve ultimate success and happiness.

Maplewood is a youth football organization outside Washington, DC, with a simple slogan: "Pride Still Matters." Taking pride in the simple and "ordinary" tasks such as blocking and tackling can lead to great accomplishments as a team both on and off the field. The same is true in life! Take great pride in every small task at the office or in your personal life. Recognize that those chores matter. The old cliché "Anything worth doing is worth doing right" has never been truer. The pride and effort we put into each task matters to someone. Even if the task does not lead to something bigger, we are still representing our company, representing our family or representing ourselves. That is our uniform.

Treat every task, large and small, as though it could make a difference in the world. It just might. *Pride still matters!*

BEWARE OF THE UNDERDOG

"You have no fear of the underdog.
That's why you will not survive!"
—Spoon

America loves a great underdog story. Overcoming long odds. Staying strong in the face of incredible adversity. Shouting down the naysayers. The underdog win is a testament to sheer will and the ultimate tribute to everyday resilience. Kurt Warner was bagging groceries in Iowa the season before leading the St. Louis Rams to the Super Bowl title. Buster Douglas was a 42-1 long shot before shocking the undefeated Mike Tyson in perhaps one of the biggest upsets in boxing history. Beyond sports, J. K. Rowling was an unemployed, single mother writing in coffee houses before her manuscript was finally picked up and the "Harry Potter" phenomenon was born. And Danny Larusso was a skinny Jersey kid with no fighting skills before he took down Johnny Lawrence and the entire Cobra Kai dojo. (Apologies. I have a thing for '80s movies!) So what does it take for an underdog to win? Hard work, perseverance, and, yes, *resilience*!

We have all been underdogs at some point in our lives. Perhaps we strived for a promotion against an incumbent with far more experience. Or pitched a sales concept against a much larger company with seemingly infinite resources. Or started a company with a great idea but no financial backing. Or even gone after the guy or girl who was way out of our league. Someone passed judgment on us and decided we should not have the job. We should not win the sale. Our company should fail. And that guy or girl should be with someone far superior to us. So how do we still move forward despite the incredible odds of failure? We simply have to *believe*.

We have to believe in the company, we have to believe in the team, and most importantly, we have to believe in ourselves. We cannot accept someone else's perception of us. They underestimate the fire and passion that is burning inside us. They underestimate our intestinal fortitude and our hunger for success. They underestimate our ability to persevere in the face of adversity. Our underdog status will fuel our quest for greatness and serve as a catalyst to achieve our ultimate goals in life. *Nobody puts Baby in a corner!* (Sorry, couldn't resist another '80s movie reference.)

But how do we maintain that edge once we have achieved our goals and reached the pinnacle of success? It is easy to relax and enjoy the moment of proving our doubters wrong. It is tempting to bask in the glory of our latest accomplishments. As we have discussed, taking time to celebrate our victories (both large and small!) is a key to happiness. But we cannot rest too long on our laurels! There is another underdog right behind us who is even hungrier for success and has even more to prove.

In my late twenties, I worked at Creative Artists Agency, a white-hot Hollywood talent agency and notorious shark tank. I once asked a young partner who had risen to the top ranks of the agency how he was able to navigate the treacherous political waters of Tinsel Town:

"Getting to the top was easy. Hard work and a little luck. Staying on top is the challenge."

And so it is with all of us. We must maintain our edge. We must stoke that fire in the belly no matter what our position in life. Circumstances change quickly and we must be prepared for the upside and the downside of fortune. *Life moves pretty fast. If we don't stop and look around once in a while, we could miss it*. Throw the flag! (I promise that will be my last '80s movie reference!)

We are in control of our own success and happiness. There will be times when no one believes in us. There will be times when we are up against incredible odds. There will be times when the deck is stacked against us and success seems unreachable. We have the ability to create our own triumphant future! Stay strong. Stay resilient. And, most importantly, beware of the underdog. Because that underdog is YOU!

WHEN IT COMES TO LEAVING A LEGACY, THINK SMALL!

"The true test of a man's character is what he does when no one is watching."
—John Wooden

When we contemplate those people who left a major legacy in this world, we tend to think on a grand scale. Michael Jordan left a legacy of greatness on the basketball court that will likely never be matched. Ray Kroc left a legacy of perseverance and vision in building McDonald's into the most iconic American brand on the planet. Marie Curie left a legacy of innovation and breakthrough research en route to claiming two Nobel Prizes for chemistry and physics. I could go on and on citing examples of towering athletic, entrepreneurial and scientific pioneers who have achieved legendary status. Their legacies are larger than life and they deserve all the accolades and respect that we thrust upon them.

But what about our legacy? We pour our soul into our craft and constantly move forward. We overcome obstacles and stay positive in the face of incredible adversity. But will anyone remember our contributions when all is said and done? The reality is, many of us will never have our statue erected in a public park or have our biographies ghost-written by a professional. We may never win a professional championship, take home a Nobel Prize, or garner an Oscar. But our work, our dreams, and our relationships are no less important.

As managers, we want to deliver maximum value to the bottom line. But our legacy will be measured by our ability to inspire the weakest member of our team. As coaches, our competitive fire drives us to win above all else. But our legacy will be measured by our ability to help the *least* athletic player maximize his or her potential. As teachers, we want to prepare our students to succeed in life at the next level. But our legacy will be built by spending extra time with the student who struggles the most. As parents, we want to keep our children safe and propel them on a path to success. But our legacy will be measured by our ability to love them even in the darkest moments.

Most legacies are not built under the white-hot spotlight or on the largest stage. They are built in quiet conversations, thoughtful reflections, and selfless acts of compassion. They are built through strong relationships, unwavering loyalty, and unconditional trust. We don't need to win an award to build a legacy. We just need to demonstrate that we genuinely care.

As we get older, we tend to get more philosophical. What will people say about us at our funeral? What have we done to change the world? Have we made a difference? *Stop worrying so much!* Any time we help someone through a difficult moment, we leave a legacy. Any time we encourage someone to pursue their dream, we leave a legacy. Any time we fight on behalf of someone else, we have left a legacy. Our legacy is growing every day in ways we do not even realize. If our passion and our ability to inspire impacts even one person, we have made this world a better place.

So, what does all this have to do with everyday resilience? If we fail to pick ourselves up and move forward, we cannot possibly help others with their goals and dreams. There is a cascading effect that negatively impacts all those in our inner circle. But staying resilient gives us purpose and allows us to build our legacy on a local level. We may not write the Great American Novel. We may not cure cancer. But our positive energy and genuine care will influence all those around us. We will inspire our family, our coworkers and our friends. And they will know we care.

Is there a better legacy?

IT'S ALL ABOUT BALANCE, RHYTHM, AND PATIENCE

"Take care not to allow one aspect of your life to so consume you, that you neglect the others."
—Coach Mike Krzyzewski

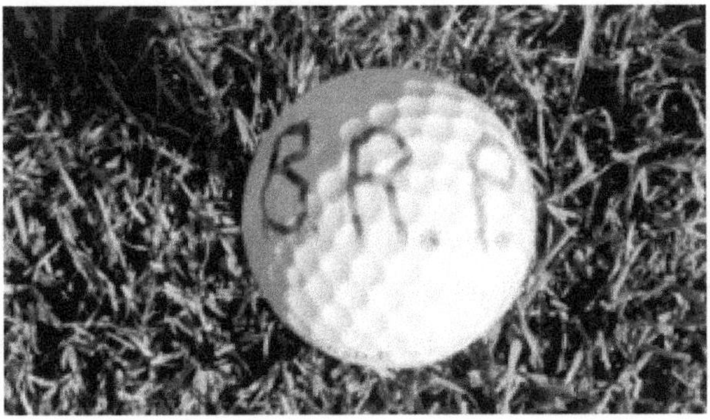

A few years back, I was playing golf with three old friends and inadvertently stumbled upon yet another valuable lesson for everyday resilience.

After striping what I *thought* was my first brilliant tee shot of the day (a blind, dogleg right approach), I walked up to the ball in the middle of the fairway and prepared for my second shot. But as I looked closer, I noticed three initials on the ball in bold marker: ***B.R.P.*** Clearly, this was not my "brilliant" tee shot. (For those of you keeping score at home, my ball was actually deep, *deep* in the woods!) Anyway, as my friend approached, I asked him about the distinct placement of the B.R.P. initials. He calmly explained the meaning:

"Balance. Rhythm. Patience. I put that on every golf ball. It is the key to a successful round."

It struck me as a perfect mantra to relax and slow things down on the golf course. And it struck me as an even more apropos reminder to strive to maintain balance, rhythm, and patience in our professional and personal lives!

If we are not careful, our work lives can quickly slide out of balance. We can maniacally push ourselves at the office at the expense of our health and family life. That is not balance. We can narrowly focus on one customer, team member, student, or player at the expense of the others. Putting all our eggs in one basket is a risky and often ineffective approach. That is not balance! To be successful, we must work hard and pour our soul into the task at hand. But we must take an even-keeled approach if we are to maintain long-term success. Establishing a formal rhythm and routine in our work life can help us stay productive and prosperous without risking burnout and loss of focus. This approach will take discipline and patience. We won't be successful overnight. But life is a marathon, not a sprint! It may take several failures and rejections before we get on the right track. If we are young, we will get there. If we are older, it is never too late. We must maintain our balance. We must establish a comfortable rhythm. And most of all, we must stay patient. Our best moments are yet to come.

The same is true in our personal lives. Are we too social and not spending enough time on our studies or work? Are we spending too much time at home in isolation instead of stretching to establish new relationships? It will take a major effort, but we must consciously strive to maintain a healthy balance between competing priorities. If we are exerting the effort to establish a consistent rhythm and routine despite the chaos, it will all work out in the end. But ultimate satisfaction in our personal life requires patience. At various points, we will turn too far to the right or too far to the left. That is okay. Balance and rhythm will be in constant flux throughout our lives. We must stay patient and keep working through the natural ebbs and flows.

This is especially true when we suffer a setback. When things get so far out of balance, hardship is inevitable. No one can escape the harsh realities that often transpire in life. But if we are to stay resilient and bounce back from these mishaps, we must be patient. We can't wallow in our misery. At the same time, we can't expect to recover immediately. Resilience requires the discipline to analyze why we failed and the courage to *move forward* despite the pain. This will take time. Everyone has some sort of struggle. We are not alone. Stay patient. Our rhythm will return. Our life will teeter back into balance. We will not stay down forever.

Balance. Rhythm. Patience. It is the key to a successful round of golf. It is the key to the young establishing themselves in this world. It is the key to the old maintaining their legacy. And most importantly for our journey, it is the key for all of us to perpetuate a passionate life of everyday resilience.

THERE ARE NO HANDOUTS!

"They are not going to GIVE us anything. We have to go out and TAKE it!"
—Coach Jim Fegan

There has been much debate recently about the intrinsic value of handouts to the needy. Some argue that it is our obligation, particularly if we have been successful, to give back to the poor in the form of food, clothing and other donations. Others argue that helping those less fortunate is inherently good, but offering handouts with no strings attached does not teach self-sufficiency and perpetuates a cycle of poverty. It is an age-old debate, and our perspective can be influenced by our politics, our economic status and our upbringing. Regardless of where we fall on this spectrum, we can all agree that idly sitting back does not help improve this world. But, ironically, when it comes to improving our own lives, many of us do sit back and passively wait for help to arrive. If we want to move our lives forward, we must take action. There are no handouts!

We all get stuck at some point in our lives. We all experience a crisis of faith that causes us to question our place in the world. Perhaps we lose confidence in our ability to execute our job. Perhaps we no longer believe in a certain cause we had espoused our entire lives. Perhaps we feel we are not maximizing our God-given potential on a daily basis. In these tough times, it is hard to look within ourselves for the right answers. Blaming others becomes the easy way out: If only my company would pay for more training, then I would be more effective in my job. If only I didn't have all these family obligations, then I could be more productive at work. Conversely, if only I didn't have all these mindless tasks at work, then I could spend more quality time with my family.

Human nature often gravitates toward excuses and shies away from accountability. The reality is that we are the ones who hold the keys to our success and happiness. We need to invest in our own training. We need to schedule our work tasks around family obligations. We need to take accountability for our own mistakes. Our problems are our problems. No one else is going to solve them for us. There are no handouts!

This is especially true when we suffer a setback. Who will help us when apathy sets in on the job front? Who will help us when stagnation sets in on the home front? Who will help us when we lose our job or fall behind on our mortgage? If we have lived a balanced, outward-focused life, we should have a close network of friends and family who can provide a safety net. Financial help, emotional support and spiritual guidance are absolutely critical during these difficult times. This type of relief is life-sustaining, and we simply could not go on without it.

But as precious as this support is in our moment of need, it is not a panacea for everything that is wrong with our lives. Ultimately, we have to take responsibility and solve our own problems. We have to find meaning and purpose in our work lives. We have to dig deep to rediscover passion in our home lives. We have to saddle up and meet our own financial obligations. Resilience is born from struggles and setbacks. But no one can be resilient for us. There are no handouts!

We are destined to do great things with our lives. It's time to take control of our destiny and maximize our potential. We need to attack our problems. We need to pursue our goals with dogged enthusiasm. We need to play an active role in our own life. And we never have to apologize for our enthusiasm! We will fail mightily at times. But if we stay positive, stay resilient, and keep moving forward, we will eventually achieve goals we never thought possible. No one is going to live our life for us. There are no handouts!

PLAYING SCARED IS NOT AN OPTION

"Courage is being scared to death . . . but saddling up anyway."
—John Wayne

We have all been scared by someone or something at some point in our lives. *Sharks. Clowns. Zombies. Ceiling fans.* We could spend all day exploring our own personal list. Fear is a powerful human emotion and can paralyze even the most stouthearted person. There is no shame in experiencing this phenomenon as there is no shortage of terrifying experiences in this world. Generally, this type of fear is temporary and subsides once the initial adrenaline rush wears off. But fear of failure is an entirely different matter. This type of fear can cause a permanent paralysis in our psyche and derail us from reaching our true potential. If we want to lead a resilient life, we must overcome this basic fear of failure.

In sports, playing with confidence is playing to win. But lack of confidence can trump athletic prowess. The running back who is afraid of getting hurt will tiptoe toward the line and go down easily. The baseball player who is afraid to swing the bat usually strikes out. In business, fear of failure leads to inaction, which dooms even the most talented executive. Once a manager stops taking risks or refuses to take a stance altogether, success becomes a pipe dream. This paralysis ensures he or she will never emerge from the pack and reach his or her personal and financial potential.

Fear of failure can impact our personal lives as well. In our relationships, this fear of failure can stifle communication or even prevent a relationship from ever forming. Expressing our emotions or asking someone out comes with an unbearable downside if we are afraid to fail. And this fear often leads to a lonely life devoid of emotion. In almost all cases, inaction due to fear of failure is a self-fulfilling prophecy. We cannot achieve happiness without expressing confidence and attacking our fears through action.

If the running back slams into the pile with confidence, he may get hurt. But he is much more likely to inflict the pain and move the ball forward with success. If the baseball player swings, he may strike out. But he will never hit a home run with the bat resting on his shoulder. The enterprising business executive may take a major revenue hit by exploring a tangential market opportunity. But "staying the course" in a down market has no chance of achieving business growth. Saying "I love you" and hearing crickets on the other side can be devastating. But better to get your heart stomped on than to have it slowly wither away!

Even the most confident people have their moments of self-doubt. It is a natural part of the human experience. But we can build our confidence by *actively* taking steps to move our lives forward. Even if it does not work out, we have proven that fear will never paralyze us or stifle our emotions. And that comforting thought will help us lead a life of confidence and action!

We will all fail. We will all suffer some type of defeat. But if we suffer that loss at full speed, we have nothing to fear. Our life will not be defined by the number of great moments versus the number of dark moments. So much in life is out of our control. But we can control our *effort*. We can control our *attitude*. Ultimately, our ability to overcome the difficult moments and actively move forward will define us. That is everyday *resilience*!

Saddle up! Go all out and fear nothing! In the end, the only failure in life is the failure to *overcome* our fear of failure.

Playing scared is NOT an option!

WEAR YOUR HEART ON YOUR SLEEVE

"Cover bands don't change the world.
Find your own unique voice."
—Todd Henry

The one thing you can count on in the Washington, DC, area is traffic. Congestion along the major arteries in and around our nation's capital is as inevitable as death and taxes. Having taken my fair share of lumps over the years, I have had far too long to read countless bumper stickers while stuck in traffic. Political affiliation. School pride. Religious denomination. Sports allegiance. Family dynamics. You can learn a lot about a driver by paying attention to their bumper stickers.

Social media allows for open communication to a potentially massive audience. But the old-school medium of billboard space on our car bumper is perhaps the most direct method of communication in society today. Where else can we learn, in an instant, that the person in front of us has two children and one dog, roots for the Redskins, vacations in the Outer Banks, runs in marathons, stands for peace and loves Jesus? Regardless of how we feel about their various affiliations, we must give these folks some credit. They are not afraid to put themselves out there!

And couldn't we all stand to do a little more of that in our own lives?

At work, how many times have we swallowed hard and toed the company line even if it conflicted with our personal views? How many times have we stifled our own ideas for fear of rejection by management? How many times have we tempered our enthusiasm in front of the client in order to look more "corporate"?

There is a time and place for everything, and we don't have to go overboard. Sometimes, we have to fall in line and put on a brave face for the rest of the office. Sometimes, our ideas need to take a backseat for the moment to let another idea germinate. Sometimes, we need to play it close to the vest with our emotions in a sales situation. But this should not be the standard operating procedure!

We need to voice our ideas. We can't throw shackles on our passion. No one is going to fault us for showing incredible effort and expressing emotion. Even if the execution is a little off, enthusiasm and passion will make up for any tactical shortcomings. We can't be afraid to let our "outside voice" overcome our "inside voice." As Walt Whitman so eloquently stated (via *Dead Poet's Society*), "I sound my barbaric YAWP over the rooftops of the world!" Let that YAWP be a positive force. Sound it out with enthusiasm. And don't let anyone take that YAWP away from you.

Imagine Dave Grohl holding back on his vocals. Or Tony Robbins sleepwalking his way through a seminar. Or Samuel Jackson mailing in a dramatic performance. There are people who let their emotions shine through in all they do. And it makes a difference. I am not suggesting we need to deliver fire and brimstone in every aspect of our lives. Not everyone is that type of person (and that is a good thing). But we need to be true to our own voice. There is no reason to stifle our ideas. Sometimes we need to shake the trees in order to feel alive.

If we are going to lead a resilient life, there are times when we have to take a close look in the mirror. How can I bounce back from my defeat? How can I build lasting relationships? How can I feel better about my contributions to this world? Most of the time, it comes down to emotion and enthusiasm. Let's pour our soul into everything we do. Let's be a shining example of passion and show conviction in all our actions. There is no downside to living a genuine life of passion and expression. Our true voice will win out in the end.

Let's not be afraid to wear our heart on our sleeve and put ourselves out there.

JUMP ON IN . . . THE WATER IS PERFECT!

"Action may not always bring happiness; but there is no happiness without action."
—Benjamin Disraeli

For some people, getting into the swimming pool is a dramatic, drawn-out affair. They dip their toe in, and then back up. Then they splash a little water on their legs, and towel off. Then they "boldly" put their whole foot underwater. Then they crisscross their arms, throw some more water on their back and start to slowly wade in. An eternity later, they finally dunk their head underwater and complete the ritual. This may be a good strategy for easing into the cold water. But when it comes to pursuing our dreams and exploring our passion, we need to jump right in!

In business, we may create an innovative sales strategy or uncover a new target market. The idea appears great on paper and we talk about it in team meetings and discuss it in focus groups. But if we never put this idea or strategy into action, we are just splashing about in the water. We may dream even bigger and consider starting our own company. We do our research and monitor the business landscape to understand the potential market. This is prudent. But eventually we have to throw all caution to the wind and dive right in! If we are too measured and careful, the opportunity could vanish as we slowly wade in.

How will we ever realize our potential if we spend our day dipping our toes in the water? If we are going to be successful, we must quickly move from theory to action. We only have a finite window to make an impact on this world. Jump on in and make it happen!

The same can be true in our personal lives. It is important to plan and think and dream. This is a cathartic exercise and (as a bonus) it separates us from the apes. But in the end we have to take action. Dreaming about playing the guitar? Stop "jamming out" on your tennis racket and go take a lesson. Considering asking someone out on a date? If we wait for just the right moment, someone else will beat us to it. Thinking about telling someone we love them? If we don't say it, that person may never know. Been meaning to run a marathon? Listening to the theme song from *Rocky* isn't going to carry us across that finish line. We need to hit the pavement.

If we want to achieve our goals and lead a fulfilling life, we must *act* on our thoughts, plans and dreams! The temperature of the water is never going to be ideal. The timing is never going to be perfect. We have a window of opportunity for every goal in our life. If we don't jump right in, we might miss our chance. So we can't be afraid to *dive in* and build our own legacy.

But what happens if we jump in and the water is freezing? We will look foolish shivering in the deep end and frantically jumping out for our warm towel. This is a legitimate risk and an uncomfortable outcome. But this is where our resilience kicks in.

We may start a business that ultimately fails. But there is a saying in the start-up world that if you are going to fail, *fail fast*! That will allow us to learn from the experience and quickly move on to the next successful venture. We could try a musical instrument and discover we have no talent. At least we had the experience and can move on to another instrument. We could ask someone out and get rejected. At least we know that person wasn't right for us. By moving on, we are one step closer to finding our soul mate.

If we never explore our passion or act on our dreams (no matter how big or small), we can never experience the sheer adrenaline of taking a chance. We can never know the thrill of achieving our goals and reaching our potential. Even if the water is too uncomfortable for us to bear, there is still a certain satisfaction gleaned from the experience. Our setbacks and failures will not keep us down forever. Our confidence will build because we have given everything we have in our quest for greatness. And, win or lose, that is what it is like to truly LIVE!

We can't wait for the ideal moment to explore our dreams and passion. We will be dipping our toes in the water forever. Take action! Stay positive! Stay resilient! Jump on in with both feet and make it happen.

Don't worry, the water is *perfect*!

EVERYDAY RESILIENCE PROFILE ON PASSION: MEET MAUREEN APPEL

Maureen Keller Appel learned early in life that education is a gift. And through all her setbacks and triumphs, she dedicated the rest of her life to instilling that education in others.

Maureen Appel grew up in a loving household in Oyster Bay, New York, as the oldest of five siblings. Her mother worked hard on the home front, and her father toiled long hours at his job as the chairman and co-founder of State Bank of Long Island. However, neither were college graduates, and they did not feel that a college education, especially for a girl, was a necessity. Maureen's grandmother, however, felt differently. So as Maureen prepared for an uncertain future in her senior year at Holy Child Academy in Old Westbury, NY, her grandmother, Nellie O'Toole, an Irish immigrant, intervened.

"She told me not to listen to my parents. She implored me to go to college."

It was a seminal moment in Maureen's life and a historic moment in the Keller family. Buoyed by this confidence, Maureen dedicated herself to her studies and vowed to continue her education at the next level. Upon graduation, Maureen was accepted to the all-girls Rosemont College in Rosemont, Pennsylvania. She would be the first person in the Keller family lineage to attend college!

Maureen continued her relentless pursuit of education. She flourished at Rosemont and developed a passion for classical language, ultimately majoring in English. But she wasn't done with her studies. From Rosemont, she went on to C.W. Post to pursue her master's in education.

"I loved my time in college and post-grad, but as I headed out into the real world, things got a little bumpy."

Maureen spent a brief stint as a manager in a Friendly's restaurant. She then pivoted through a family connection to do some accounting work at Genovese Drugs. But neither job lit her on fire.

"I realized how much I missed the education system."

After a few years of struggling, Maureen finally returned to the classroom. She received an offer to teach eighth-grade English at nearby St. Aidan's School. She absolutely loved it. But that didn't mean it was without its challenges.

"I was so naive. On the first day, I put on a beautiful green dress. A few boys placed gum on my chair and I sat right down in the middle of it. I didn't get up for the rest of the lesson!"

Pranks aside, Maureen spent five wonderful years at the school. But the best part of her life's journey was about to begin.

"A May-December Romance!"

Maureen was volunteering at a function for widowed spouses when she met Thomas Appel. Thomas was a widower with five children, in addition to five adopted children from a previous marriage. Two of the children were older than Maureen. But it was love at first sight.

"I was young, but sometimes you just know. And I knew."

After only six months of dating, they were married. The

newlyweds made such a unique and compelling couple, their courtship was featured on the nationally televised *Phil Donahue Show* under the episode title "A May to December Romance."

"That was a real thrill. I knew we had something special."

Thomas was a successful land developer, which allowed Maureen to stay home and manage the household. But Maureen discovered something during her time away from work.

"I didn't like it. I missed the schools and wanted to get back out there."

At roughly the same time, the 1982 recession took a financial toll on Thomas's real estate ventures. By early 1983, Maureen was actively interviewing to get back in the job market. During her time at St. Aidan's, many colleagues had encouraged her to move into the administration side of the education system. And, as fate would have it, the director of development position opened up at her alma mater, Holy Child Academy.

The following years were golden for the Appel family. Maureen embraced her role at Holy Child and grew personally and professionally. In addition, she hosted a show on local Cable Channel 12 ("Today's Family") about modern families in the New York area.

"Tom was always so supportive of my public speaking both in front of the camera and at the school events. He really built up my self-esteem."

And speaking of family, the Appels added to their own family during these years. Daughter Jaci followed by son Tyler completed the circle.

"It was a precious time."

But after eleven years at the school, Maureen was ready to take the next step in her career. She had both the educational background and the fundraising skills to run a school. She thought she would spend the rest of her life in New York. But out of the blue, she received a call from Enos Fry, vice chairman of Connelly School of the Holy Child's Board of Trustees in Potomac, Maryland. They were looking for a head of school. It was a great opportunity for Maureen, but it was also a huge stretch.

"I had never run an entire school before. And, frankly, I had never heard of Potomac, Maryland!"

But she responded to the call and met with Enos at Congressional Country Club shortly thereafter. Maureen could not have been more impressed. The following week she met with Len Ralston, the chairman of the board and the search committee at Holy Child. A few days later, Maureen received a phone call from Sr. Helen McDonald, SHCJ, who offered her the job. She was overjoyed.

"It was fabulous! The education of young women was important to me. And I felt so welcome in this new community."

But Jaci was now in seventh grade and had her friends and way of life. Tyler was only five years old and just settling into school. Moving the entire family would create upheaval in their lives.

"It was not without its challenges. But every change in life comes with a tradeoff."

Amen, Maureen!

In the early summer of 1994, the Appel family relocated from New York to Potomac, Maryland. It was the best move of their lives.

The (Potomac) Holy Child Years

Maureen and her family moved into a beautiful white house right in the middle of Holy Child's campus. This was her new home and it was time to get started with her mission. But little did she realize the challenges in front of her.

In one of her first meetings, Maureen realized there was barely enough money in the school budget to make payroll.

"I had never read a bank statement before. That was a real eye-opener. I realized I needed to sharpen my skills and act quickly."

The first few months were a baptism by fire. But Maureen was comfortable asking for money, having spent eleven years as a director of development. She poured her energy into the financial side of the school. She hosted fundraisers in the community. She went out to the local elementary schools and spread the word about Holy Child. She raised the pay for teachers to attract the best and the brightest. After a couple of years, the school was out of danger and on solid financial ground.

At the same time, the family moved out of the white house on campus to a nearby house right behind the school.

"It was the perfect place to raise the children and host events. Our entire family was part of the Holy Child community. And I will never forget our Sunday dinners at the old house. All of us together."

With the family secure, Maureen found time for two additional pursuits. First she continued her education at Johns Hopkins, completing a post-master's graduate degree in "Adolescents at Risk."

"As the head of school at an all-girls high school, I can't tell you how valuable it was to gain that perspective."

The second pursuit had an impact on the school that still stands today. Maureen has never been able to hear out of her left ear. As a result of this condition, she had more difficulty learning than most children. It took some major adjustments just to keep up.

"Having gone through that experience, I always had an appreciation for those students who needed more support."

Inspired by this, Maureen started the Academic Support Center at Holy Child, which has helped hundreds of students adjust and acclimate to a new learning environment.

With the school stabilized and the curriculum in place, it was time to launch a development strategy at Holy Child. With the board of directors by her side, Maureen embarked on a $17 million capital campaign to renovate the school and add a major new building to the campus.

It required focus and discipline. But the entire community rallied behind the cause. And the seminal moment came a year later when

Maureen and her family traveled to Kerry, Ireland, to meet with Sr. Pauline McShain, SHCJ. She pledged $500,000 to the campaign and agreed to fulfill her pledge in two payments. That act of generosity provided the final piece to the puzzle. A beautiful new building, Connelly Hall, was built on the spot of the old white house on campus. Mission accomplished!

And as the years rolled on, there were more challenges and triumphs. The community lived through the devastating September 11th attacks. They endured twenty-three harrowing days in October 2002 when a sniper was on the loose in the Washington, DC, area. And the Appel family continued to grow up and grow together.

The Sunday family dinners continued. Jaci eventually went on to Holy Child (a shortcut through her backyard) and Tyler to Georgetown Prep High School.

During this whole time5, Thomas was a stay-at-home dad. He attended every event, every game, and every meeting at Holy Child. He was a fixture in the community. And he continued to support Maureen's public speaking and leadership. He was her rock.

"I couldn't have done any of this without him. He was so supportive and he loved Holy Child beyond words."

But the Appel family was about to find out how fragile life could be.

A Sudden Tragedy

June 14, 2008, is a day forever ingrained in the hearts of the Appel family. Maureen had just finished up her fourteenth year at Holy Child. Tyler had just graduated from Georgetown Prep a few weeks before, and Jaci was out in the working world.

Thomas Appel played eighteen holes at Congressional Country Club that day and still had time for a lesson afterwards. He was tired that evening and went to bed early. In the middle of the night, Thomas suffered a massive brain aneurysm. He never woke up.

It was a shock beyond description to the Appel family.

"I never imagined my life without him."

And it was a further shock to the extended Washington, DC, community, who showed up in droves to attend the funeral at Holy Trinity Church. All twelve of Thomas's children were together in one place. The atmosphere was incredible.

"It was the most uplifting service I have ever attended. There was a rock band that played beautiful music, and so many people poured their hearts out in support. It was unforgettable."

And there was one more unforgettable moment. After stirring eulogies from Tyler and two of Thomas's older sons, Maureen stood up, walked to the front of the church, and delivered an impromptu eulogy.

"It wasn't in the program. But Tom was always so supportive of my public speaking. A feeling came over me in the moment. I wanted to honor him by making him proud one more time."

And so she did.

The Appel family struggled with confusion and grief in the ensuing months. But there was one silver lining.

"It made us all so much closer. We saw how fragile life could be and we appreciated our moments together that much more. To this day, Jaci and Tyler are so close as a result."

Life marches on, and they had to pick up the pieces.

"We carried on but a lot of the fun was gone. Thank goodness for the support of the Holy Child community."

But after a few years, Maureen didn't have the same passion. She was out of the big house and living alone in an apartment in nearby Chevy Chase, MD. The technology had changed. Phones and distractions were more prevalent in the classroom. It was time. After twenty years as head of school at Holy Child, Maureen Appel stepped down.

"I was not sure what I was going to do next. Educational consulting was certainly an option, but I felt it would be too isolating after the hustle and bustle of running a school. But I knew I just had to keep going.

A Change of Scenery

In 2014, Maureen moved to the suburbs of Boston to become president of Notre Dame Academy in Tyngsboro, Massachusetts.

"It was cold up there and I didn't know a soul. But I made it work."

Maureen loved her new community, but it was an adjustment moving from the comfort of Washington, DC. She persevered and made the most of her experience. After two years, she received a surprise call from her nephew. There was an opening at St. Dominic's School in her old hometown of Oyster Bay. It was an opportunity to return to family.

"I was excited to get the call. But I told my nephew that they would never hire a sixty-year-old to run the school."

But they did. And Maureen Appel was back home.

"Once I got there, I thought I would never leave. I was positive this was the end of the road."

But after three years, Maureen had grown increasingly disillusioned with the Church in the wake of the sex abuse scandals with the clergy in Washington. Fate once again intervened.

In March 2019, she received another out-of-the-blue offer. This time it was from Eddie Quinn, chairman of the board at San Miguel School in Silver Spring, MD. She decided to at least hear him out.

San Miguel is an all-boys middle school dedicated to transforming lives for academically and economically disadvantaged Latino youth. Maureen traveled back down to the DC area and was *absolutely* blown away by the mission and the purpose of the school.

"Everyone was so gracious. And the faculty was simply amazing."

But it was the students who ultimately swayed Maureen.

"Eighty-two percent of the students were below the poverty line. But they were perfectly attired and behaved. I left the school in absolute tears. They were a blessing."

The San Miguel community had transformed Maureen. The fire was back. The head of school was on the move once again

A Renewed Passion

Maureen moved back to the DC area and started at San Miguel on July 1, 2019. It has been a labor of love ever since.

"I now realize you can only ask for money if you have the passion. And I have never been more passionate. I just want to put the boys in the best position."

Maureen soon came to understand the intense rigor of the program. The school day lasts from 8 a.m. to 5 p.m., and the boys are in class from August to June. And reading is a major focus to break the cycle of poverty. The San Miguel boys are required to read forty books a year!

"The boys appreciate the opportunity so much. They helped me understand that education is a gift."

And perhaps more importantly, the San Miguel experience has helped renew Maureen's faith in the Church.

"They won my heart. And I now see God working through them."

Maureen Appel's transformation was complete. But nothing can take the place of family.

Now that she is back in the Washington, DC, area, Maureen is reunited with her family and has renewed the Sunday evening tradition of dinner with Jaci and Tyler.

"In this frenetic world, it is so important to pick a time to appreciate one another."

And eleven years after the passing of their father, Jaci and Tyler remain as close as ever.

"Tyler recently got married to a wonderful girl, Emily, and Jaci served as his best man. Imagine that. I am so thankful."

And there you have it. A resilient journey. A renewed passion. An appreciation for family. And a lifetime dedicated to education.

Maureen Appel's journey has not been without its struggles.

There have been tough decisions, heartbreak, tumultuous moves, and uncertainty. But her resilience has carried her through. And the world is a better-educated and more loving place as a result.

What a gift, indeed!

Appreciation

"Don't forget, a person's greatest emotional need is to feel appreciated."
—Jackson Brown

WINNING THE LOTTERY

"Develop an attitude of gratitude and give thanks for everything in your life."
—Brian Tracy

Bam! You just won the latest Powerball jackpot! $200 million coming your way. Congrats! Now, what are you going to do with all that money?

This is an age-old question, pondered by the young and old as they daydream of untold riches and an opulent lifestyle. Typical answers involve acquiring more "stuff." Buying a boat, plane, private island, beach house or mansion. Sounds like a plan.

But a conversation with a trusted client offered a remarkably refreshing perspective on winning the lottery. My client keeps a list of all the people who have helped him in his life. Family members. Loved ones. Colleagues. Mentors. Old friends. He calls it his **"Lottery List."**

If he strikes it big with six matching numbers, he will pay his Lottery List first. How? Cash gift cards with a monthly stipend up to the maximum amount, refillable in perpetuity. *That works!*

I asked him about updating the list, potentially pruning it as he moves through the different stages of his life.

"It's not about taking people off the list. Just because I'm not currently in touch with someone doesn't mean I have forgotten about them. It's more about meeting new people and *adding* them to the list."

The Lottery List is one of the simplest and most powerful manifestations of *appreciation*. My client recognizes that he couldn't get to where he is now without help. *So true.* We can't make it alone. We have to cherish those who inspire us, encourage us, and make our lives better. And while this is a noble concept as it pertains to the lottery, we should keep this perspective in mind *at all times*.

In our work and personal lives, we need to recognize and appreciate our "Lottery List," even if we never buy a single ticket.

In our work lives, it takes a village to reach any level of success. The founder of a company can't bring his vision to life without a dedicated and loyal staff to see it through. The all-star salesperson can't achieve rainmaker status without help from research or technical support. The manager can't make an impact on the company without team members who sacrifice for the cause. The coach or teacher will never be fulfilled unless their players and students put in the work. We are all interconnected and we need to recognize we are not on an island.

That is not to say that *our own toil and unique talent* play no role in our own success. Quite the contrary! We have earned the rewards of our hard work. We deserve to celebrate our victories. But our Lottery List of support also deserves our attention. They deserve our recognition. They deserve our loyalty in return. And when the time comes to show our gratitude, they deserve to know how much they mean to us.

And this is even more critical in our personal lives. Who are the people that have earned that first cut of the lottery money? The parent who always has our back. The son or daughter who returns the love later in life. The brother or sister who is always there for us in our time of need. The friend who always shoots straight. The spouse who offers unconditional love. Where would we be without these people?

There are times when the tidal wave of stress washes over us. There are times when it feels as if we are drowning. There are times when we feel all alone with the struggle. But we are not alone. We are never alone. Our inner circle will always be there for us. Our loved ones who guided us through the difficult times will ALWAYS be on our list. They deserve to know how much we care. They deserve to share in the spoils of any "riches" that come our way.

And sometimes *appreciation* is the greatest and only gift we can offer.

We need to make our list. We need to keep these people in the forefront of our minds. Without our Lottery List, we wouldn't have a career. Without our Lottery List, we wouldn't survive our everyday struggles. Without the people on our Lottery List, we wouldn't be able to stay *resilient*!

So go ahead and buy that lottery ticket if you are in the mood. Financial analysts will tell you it is not a wise investment. They are probably correct. But why not dream a little? Just don't be disappointed if it doesn't go your way. There is more to the lottery than matching all six numbers.

Make your Lottery List. Keep adding to it. That list holds the key to your success and fulfillment. And that list is the greatest jackpot of all.

Cherish those people on your Lottery List. If you stay true to them and show your appreciation, you don't need to check your numbers. You have already won!

JENGA PIECES IN YOUR LIFE

"There are no extra pieces in the universe. Everyone is here because he or she has a place to fill, and every piece must fit itself into the big jigsaw puzzle."
—Deepak Chopra

My wife and I are constantly searching for creative ways to spend time with our four children. Other than watching *SpongeBob* (the great communicator across ALL generations), it is becoming increasingly difficult to find common ground. Years ago, we stumbled upon the game Jenga, and it seems to have satisfied our criteria for effective family entertainment: no groans when we suggest the game, and no tears when it is all over.

For those not familiar with Jenga, players take turns removing one block from a tower constructed of fifty-four blocks. Each block removed is then balanced on top of the tower, creating a progressively taller but less stable structure. When a player removes a critical supporting piece, and the tower falls down, that player loses, and everyone screams "Jenga!" (some louder than others). In the game of Jenga, one never knows which piece, when removed, will cause the entire tower to collapse. Clearly, some pieces are more critical to the stability of the tower and others can be removed without any disturbance to the overall structure.

In the same way, our lives are full of Jenga pieces. In order to maintain our happiness and success, we need to recognize which pieces are critical to our overall stability. In our personal lives, which relationships, if lost or strained, will cause major upheaval and heartache? Perhaps it is a spouse that provides bedrock support or motivation to keep it all together. Perhaps it is a parent that always provides that timely advice or understanding to stave off an inevitable collapse.

As salespeople, we need to recognize which customers, if lost, will have major negative financial consequences on our portfolio. Perhaps they are not the largest, but they are influencers or pioneers that believe in our product and attract other customers. As managers, it is critical to understand which employees, if lost, will cause the rest of the team to disperse or underperform. Perhaps it is not even a top producer. Recognize that attitude is critical to the dynamic of your organization and retain those workers that serve as the glue for the team.

As business owners, we must recognize which partnerships, if dissolved, will cause the rest of the enterprise to come tumbling down. Does the partnership give us the best chance to succeed? Does it align with our mission? (Fact: The best partnerships are usually about more than revenue). Understanding which areas of our business and our life we need to protect and develop is an incredibly valuable skill. Give it some critical thought and do not take this lightly. Our happiness and survival are at stake!

But sometimes things are not always what they seem. Some pieces appear to be important, but, when removed, have little impact on our life. There is a lot of sizzle in both our personal lives and our business lives. Relationships which start out exciting and fun can end up shallow and pointless. Salespeople can beat their chest about how much they bring to the bottom line, when, in fact, they deliver little value to their clients or the team. Partnerships can look great on paper but ultimately have minimal impact, or even a negative impact on our bottom line. These pieces can all be removed without any damage to the structure of our life or our organization. The sooner we recognize this, the sooner we can focus on the pieces that *truly* matter.

How can we tell the difference between the critical pieces and the ones that can easily be removed? Unfortunately, it takes a lot of trial and error. Sometimes, we will let a close relationship collapse. Learn from it and rebuild that relationship or go out and build a new one. Sometimes, we let a key employee get away (to another company or another career). Recognize the qualities of that person, and do not let it happen in the future. Sometimes, we dissolve a business partnership that provided major revenue. Move on and go search out the next great partnership. As long as we learn from our mistakes, it becomes much easier to recognize the Jenga pieces in our life.

The worst case scenario is not so bad. As devastating as it is when that tower collapses, remember that you can always rebuild! Life, like Jenga, is a never-ending game. The destruction and chaos is only temporary. We need to keep building our tower. We need to learn from our mistakes and focus on the truly important pieces in our life. Above all else, we must summon the strength to keep playing! We will only get better if we keep moving forward. That is Jenga. That is life. That is everyday resilience!

IT'S TIME TO FORGET REGRET

"I'd rather regret the things I've done, than regret the things I haven't done."
—Lucile Ball

We all have moments in our lives we wish we could go back and change. Perhaps a fork in the road not taken, a rash decision, or a life-changing event from the past still nibbles away at our soul. If only we had a time machine to travel back and make a different decision or action. If only we could wipe away that regret. What an incredible impact that would have on our future! This regret is perhaps the biggest obstacle to happiness and success. And it is a powerful enemy to everyday resilience.

Regret can paralyze even the most optimistic person, and it eventually leads to bitterness and self-doubt. Even worse, regret can rob us of the present moment and cause us to live life in the rearview mirror. This is not a winning formula for a meaningful life! If we want to stay resilient and move forward with our lives, we need to learn how to forget regret.

In my twenties and early thirties, I chased several business opportunities that I thought would set me on a path to financial independence. I worked hard, kept the faith, and persevered through some difficult times. While rewarding in other ways, none of those opportunities translated into major financial success. At the same time, many of the jobs I passed on turned out to be incredibly lucrative (for others!). I have spent way too much time regretting those outcomes. How could I turn down those opportunities? What would my life be like if I had made the "right" choices? If only I could jump in that aforementioned time machine and take another path.

While regret will always play some role in our lives, there are ways to minimize the impact and move forward with resilience. First, it is important to realize that the time machine cuts both ways. Yes, it would be nice to jump back and reverse certain decisions in our lives. But what would we be giving up? If I had taken another job, would I still have married my wife? Would I have four beautiful children? Would I have made the same type of friends as I did at the other companies I chose? I would not risk any of those to make a different decision. Furthermore, there is no guarantee the other "lucrative" jobs would have worked for me. Perhaps I would have hated the experience and quit or been bounced out. Once we understand and *appreciate* all the blessings we currently have in our life, it is much easier to deal with the regret of a "wrong" decision from the past.

In addition, the effort we put into our present life makes regret much more tolerable. In my case, I still worked hard and gave everything I had on the opportunities that did not pan out. When we believe in something and stay passionate, there is an overwhelming feeling that something good is bound to happen. That gives us great hope for the future. Success will eventually find those that work hard and keep a positive attitude.

But what if we have not been giving 100 percent? We all experience work fatigue, apathy or frustration at some point in our careers. What if we have settled into a comfortably numb career filled with regret over things that might have been? The good news is, it is never too late to move forward! That time machine isn't coming (and if it did, would you really want it?), so rather than stew about the past, start creating your own future!

Forget regret and feel the exhilaration and excitement of a fresh beginning. Success and fulfillment are right around the corner. We need to stop looking back in the rearview mirror and start looking forward to our next great accomplishment. Our path to everyday resilience lies ahead!

I GOT YOUR BACK

"I believe that the most meaningful way to succeed is to help other people succeed."
—Adam Grant

Urban Dictionary defines "Got Your Back" as follows: *An expression assuring someone that you are watching out for them. Comes from making someone feel safe by watching what's behind them when they're busy looking ahead.*

We all know and appreciate people in our lives who have had our back in various ways. And there is no greater expression of loyalty than assuring we have someone else's back in return. Perhaps the best example of this happens in the military. A tight platoon of soldiers has each other's back and ensures everyone in their company is safe. In turn, collectively, they have our nation's back and keep us safe while we are looking ahead. These soldiers put the needs of our country ahead of their own individual needs even if it means paying the ultimate price. At its core, that is why our military is so honored and revered in this country.

As managers in the workplace, we have to adopt this same mentality. If we want to engender loyalty, trust, and unity within our team, we need to demonstrate the ability to put our employees' needs above our own. Stepping in to help close a deal without taking credit. Fighting to gain extra compensation for a team member even if it will not directly benefit us. Allowing extra time off for a team member who may be caring for a sick parent or spouse. This demonstration of selflessness and compassion pays huge dividends on both the personal and business fronts. Most employees hunger and thirst for real leadership. And, unfortunately, it seems to be in diminishing supply in corporate America. But the highest-performing teams have leaders who demonstrate—through actions, not words—care for their employees above their own self-interests. That is why team members are willing to run through brick walls in order to deliver results for these types of leaders. If we truly have our team's back, we will be repaid with a level of productivity and personal satisfaction we never thought possible.

The same is true in our personal lives. Putting the needs of our family above our own is critical to ensuring that the entire unit survives. We all work hard so our children can receive a proper education and live a comfortable life. That is the American Dream. But we also have to ensure that our children, spouse, brothers, sisters, parents and other family members know we have their back in other ways.

In my pre-teen years, I would *occasionally* get in trouble at school. I still remember one afternoon when I was blamed for something I didn't do (I swear!) and was sent home from school for the day. As I trudged toward our house, I felt as if no one was in my corner and no one had my back. What an incredibly lonely feeling! But all that changed as I walked up our front steps. My mom immediately opened the door, gave me a hug and told me she believed me and would always be there for me. *Thanks for having my back, Mom!*

There is nothing more critical to our happiness and success than our trusted group of friends and family who have our back.

And there is nothing more important than repaying those people by ensuring that we will always have their back in return.

It is nearly impossible to lead a resilient life without leaning on these close relationships both at home and in the office. Resilience is not something that happens in a vacuum. We cannot "go it alone" when things are falling apart all around us. We need someone to watch our back so we can keep moving forward. The smallest gesture of loyalty or support from a family member or colleague can turn a disaster into a mere bump in the road.

Think about the people who have helped us through the difficult times. Is there anything we wouldn't do for them? At the same time, think about how many people we have supported in their moment of need. It doesn't go unnoticed.

Our military is predicated upon loyalty, selfless service and courage. We need to demonstrate those same values in our personal and professional lives to ensure we continue to live in a resilient world.

Stay strong! Stay loyal! And don't worry if things don't go as planned. *Someone will always have our back.*

YOUR PARACHUTE HAS BEEN PACKED WITH CARE

"It's okay to have personal ambitions, but you have to take someone with you."
—Roger Staubach

This is the story of Captain Charlie Plumb, a US Navy fighter pilot who served during the Vietnam War. Capt. Plumb was shot down in enemy territory while flying on a covert mission and was forced to parachute out in mid-air as his plane disintegrated around him. He landed with minor injuries but was immediately captured by the enemy and spent nearly six years in a POW camp. After his release, Plumb became a motivational speaker, drawing on lessons from his time in captivity. But his biggest lesson came twenty years later when a stranger in a restaurant rushed out of the crowd to shake his hand.

"Are you fighter pilot Charlie Plumb?"

"Yes. How on earth did you know that?" asked Plumb.

"I was the one who packed your parachute! I guess it worked!"

Plumb was dumbfounded. He drew a few lessons from his time in captivity but never once considered the enormity and simplicity of the fact that his parachute deployed properly. Not only that, but it was someone's job to pack it with care. And that someone had saved his life. Now, twenty years later, that someone was standing right in front of him!

What a great lesson for everyday resilience. How many people in our everyday lives carefully pack our parachute so we can succeed? At work, our boss may run interference for us to make sure we are protected from the intra-office politics. The office manager may diligently order the supplies and handle the invoicing so the managers can focus on growth. In our personal lives, one spouse may take care of the children or other household duties so the other can focus on bringing home the income. Parents are constantly doing little things for their children to keep them safe and on the right path. These little things often go unnoticed and unacknowledged.

How often do we thank the people who pack our parachutes? How often do we tell them that we simply could not make it without them? Sir Edmund Hillary had Tenzing Norgay. Alexander Graham Bell had Thomas Watson. Johnny Cash had June Carter. We all have people in our lives that care for us in little ways and allow us to be successful. We need to let them know they have made a difference in our life. No one makes it to the top of the mountain alone.

At the same time, we are never alone when we fall on hard times. We may feel isolated. But if we want to lead a resilient life, we have to recognize there are people who will never leave our side. Our inner circle, whether in the office or in our personal life, will still be there for us, ready to pack our parachute. They will help us through the crisis and allow us to take on our next great challenge. Just as no one can succeed alone, no one can get through these difficult times alone. Do not be afraid to ask for help and support. The people who love us will not judge. The world wants us to be happy and succeed. We just need to appreciate those people who care enough to ensure we have a soft landing.

Whether we realize it or not, we are all walking around with parachutes. Our inner circle, who has packed them, hopes we will never need to use them. But we will. And that is okay.

Captain Charlie Plumb has provided the ultimate lesson for us. We all get shot down at some point. We all have to face tough situations. We all experience adversity and loss. But isn't it comforting to know that someone really cares? Isn't it comforting to know that our parachute will always deploy if we recognize and appreciate the little things that people do for us? Isn't it comforting to know that we can return the love and support to someone else?

Embrace all that life has to offer and do not be afraid to fail. We will land softly. Our parachute has been packed with care.

"WE'LL BE THERE FOR YOU ON YOUR WORST DAY"

"Lots of people want to ride with you in the limo, but what you want is someone who will take the bus with you when the limo breaks down!"
—Oprah Winfrey

A few years ago, my friend's son navigated the college lacrosse recruiting process. He was a big, athletic player in huge demand from several reputable programs. For the most part, it was an incredibly humbling and rewarding experience.

All the schools had good intentions and described scenarios where his son would thrive in school and bask in the glory of the team's success.

"We will help you win a national championship."

"We will get you the exposure you need to be All-Conference."

"You will be the centerpiece of our program, and we have a spot for you to play right away."

This is all positive. Who doesn't want to win? Who doesn't want to have individual and team success?

But one school took a markedly different approach.

One school rose above the others and channeled unconditional support and resilience:

"We think you will be successful here, but it's not going to be easy.

"You are going to face a day when you are injured. When your girlfriend dumps you. When you aren't getting the playing time you think you deserve. When you feel like a little fish in a big pond.

"We will be there for you on your ***worst*** *day!"*

Sign me up for that school. Isn't that what life is all about?

Our careers are going to be a roller coaster. We will experience incredible thrills that we think will last forever. The market will be soaring. Our clients will be begging us for solutions. Our decisions will turn into gold. Our team will get along and crush its goal.

We will be able to share these incredible moments with our coworkers. We will have the support of management and our shareholders. Our team will respect and appreciate our leadership.

But the meteoric rise to the top will not last forever.

Markets crash. Customers disappear. Teams can bicker and self-implode. We will not always make the right decisions. Who will be there for us at our lowest moment? Who will help us pick up the pieces?

These are the people we must remember. Those are the people we must cherish. Those are the people who will help us stay resilient.

The same is true in every aspect of our lives. There will be winning streaks. There will be times of financial success. There will be times when our family members all get along. We will build strong relationships and experience harmony in our personal life.

But losing streaks happen. Expenses can drain our savings. Relationships can wither. Our family will not always be moving in the same direction.

How do we get back on track? Where can we turn?

We turn to our support group. We quickly learn who will be there for us and who is along for the ride. We seek out those special individuals who care enough to help us on our ***worst*** day.

And those who have helped us on our worst day *will be there* to celebrate on our best day.

Adversity, by its very definition, is not easy. We don't want to fail. We don't want to experience pain. We don't seek out uncomfortable and difficult moments. Nobody likes to lose.

But those losses make the victory so much sweeter. Those failures make us truly appreciate the triumphs. That pain leads to so much joy when we turn things around.

We will be rewarded by our choice to channel resilience rather than resignation!

And the celebration with those who have been there for us in down times will be so much more meaningful. The bonds will be so much stronger because they have experienced the losses with us. They have felt our pain. And now they see how far we have come. Now, they are a part of our success!

The colleges promising glory, fame and success were not wrong. We should always strive for the best. We should have goals and dreams and an optimistic outlook on our future. We should be able to picture victory.

But sustained success requires a powerful team. It requires the right environment. It requires a support system to help us when we make a mistake or choose the wrong path. It requires someone who will not abandon us when the road gets rocky.

Who is going to roll with us until the wheels fall off?

Who is going to be there for us on our ***worst*** *day?*

LEAVE SOME ROOM IN YOUR LIFE FOR HOPE

"Hope is a good thing, maybe the best of things, and no good thing ever dies."
—Andy Dufresne, *Shawshank Redemption*

Many years ago, my son's eighth-grade class put on an incredible performance of *The Shawshank Redemption*. While *Shawshank the Musical* may not be sweeping Broadway anytime soon, there was something magical about watching a group of fourteen-year-old boys act out one of the greatest stories ever told.

For those not familiar with the plotline, *Shawshank* tells the story of Andy Dufresne, a man falsely accused of murdering his wife. Sentenced to life in prison, he must deal with a violent, dead-end world without hope. After twenty years inside the crumbling walls of Shawshank Prison, his only salvation is the possibility of a daring escape. This sliver of hope allows Andy to survive in this brutal world.

It is this hope (even the faintest hope) that allows us to stay positive and motivated despite all the setbacks in our lives. I firmly believe, deep down, that people are naturally prone to optimism (*Can you tell from the tone of this book?*). Eventually, life beats this hope out of some of us and leaves a trail of pessimism and bitterness in its place. Business failures, broken relationships, financial hardship and mundane tasks can sap our positive energy.

But we can overcome all of this if we maintain the smallest kernel of hope. Hope is the possibility (not the *promise*) of better times ahead. We know there are no guarantees for future success. But just imagining a better future puts us in a state of mind to keep moving forward and fighting for a better life.

Hope means different things to different people. Is it the possibility of working our way up the corporate ladder or simply achieving financial success? Is it the possibility of dating a special person or positively impacting someone's life? Is it something even bolder?

We can't be afraid to dream big and feed off the potential for the future. Along the way, there will be people who tell us to stop wasting our time with a lofty goal. They may be well-intentioned, but it is up to us to keep hope alive. Everyone is different, and as long as our dreams, goals and actions give us hope, it is a good thing. *And no good thing ever dies.*

The enemy to hope is "never."

I could never be as strong as him.

I could never be as smart as her.

I could never write that line, throw that pass, hit that golf shot, solve that equation, play that instrument, make that speech, or run that company.

"Never" automatically takes us out of the game. We give up before we even start the race. All hope is removed and eventually we start to believe those negative voices. Apathy sets in and we don't even care if tomorrow is a better day. We just want tomorrow to come as quickly as possible so we can get it over with.

We need to snap out of it!

Hope is easy. It doesn't cost us anything. It doesn't ask anything from us. It doesn't come with a downside. And the beautiful thing is, anyone can have it. Hope comes from within.

Good managers and coaches will tell you that hope is not a strategy. And they are absolutely correct! Hope doesn't take the place of hard work, execution, and vision. Hope doesn't take the place of determination and grit. We can't just hope for a better life and then do nothing to back it up.

But sometimes we put in the effort, pay the price, execute on our plan and it still doesn't translate to success. These setbacks, both personally and professionally, can be devastating. During these times, it is that hope for the future that allows us to move forward and give it another shot. We need to put our cards on the table. We need to keep hope alive!

I hope we all find success in our next endeavor. I hope we always maintain that drive to maximize our potential. Above all else, I hope (and that is the best of things).

THE UPSIDE OF A CRISIS

"If it doesn't work out, there will never be any doubt, that the pleasure was worth all the pain."
—Jimmy Buffett

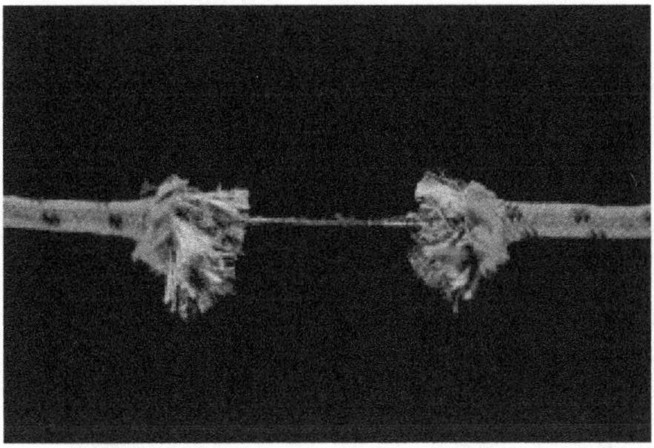

Nobody prays for a crisis. We don't wish it upon other people and we don't wish it upon ourselves. There is real pain and stress that takes a personal toll on everyone involved. The death of a loved one, a broken relationship, a setback at work, or financial hardship. In these moments, it is time to circle the wagons and deal head-on with the struggle at hand. It is also an opportunity for us to lean on our core group of friends and family who are there for us when we need it most.

Care and concern demonstrated by our inner circle in a time of crisis will never be forgotten. It is one of the "good" things to come from a setback. And the bigger the tragedy, the more we appreciate the loyalty, love and support of these relationships. Everyone is going through some type of crisis. We must help our inner circle through these difficult periods. Sympathy and understanding can turn a major catastrophe into a temporary speed bump.

In the business world, the same principle applies to our clients. In my first job out of college, I sold office supplies in the Washington, DC, area. As I was struggling to build my client base, I learned how powerful it was to help a client in crisis. An urgent need for a toner cartridge when a small business was on deadline for a project. Personal delivery of copier paper when a law firm had to file a brief on time. Rapid response and care in these mini-crises made a huge difference to these companies. While I wasn't saving the world, I was demonstrating loyalty and support when my clients needed it most. They never forgot my response in their time of need, and they became the foundation of my business for years to come.

Trust and loyalty increase exponentially if we can help someone through a crisis. While offering support in a crisis is not about getting something in return, it is imperative in our personal life and the right thing to do for our business.

In the same way, quality managers must realize that their team members are composed of individuals who occasionally go through difficult times. Managers don't need to delve into the personal lives of their team, but they should be able to recognize when extra support is needed.

Many years ago, when I moved from the West Coast to take a job in New York, I was almost completely bankrupt. The cross-country move coupled with the expensive Manhattan rent created a major drain on my finances. To make matters worse, there was a glitch in the payroll system and I did not get my paycheck for the first full month of employment. I had no way to pay the rent, much less buy groceries.

Panic was setting in and I had nowhere to turn. My boss, Dave Gwozdz, did not know how dire my personal situation was, but he intuitively sensed that this glitch would be problematic for me. He called me into his office and offered me $500 cash to pay my rent. (I told you this was a long time ago!) He refused to take no for an answer and refused to let me pay him back. What a selfless and empathetic gesture!

While $500 was not a lot of money for him, it meant the world to me. It also engendered incredible trust and loyalty. I worked as hard as I possibly could for him and never forgot his act of generosity. To this day, I would drop everything to take his call. Coming through for a team member in a crisis, while a reward in its own right, can set us apart as a manager and a friend.

We cannot wish for a life free from crisis. This will only lead to disappointment. Instead, we need to focus on the love of our inner circle of friends and family who *will* support us in our own time of need. And pray for the strength to return the favor when our support is needed.

What more can we ask for in a time of crisis?

WHAT WILL PEOPLE SAY ABOUT US AT OUR FUNERAL?

"To live in the hearts we leave behind is not to die."
—Thomas Campbell

I have attended a fair number of funerals in my day, and it always amazes me how the eulogists can deliver such insightful and eloquent remarks in their time of grief. In these remembrances, we are presented with a window into the remarkable legacy of the deceased. The eulogy also serves the dual purpose of honoring a tremendous life while easing the pain of those left to mourn. There is something beautiful and poetic about offering the final testimony of our journey here on earth. If there is ever a time for ultimate perspective, this is the moment. Too bad we won't be around to witness it!

So why not live our lives with this final perspective in mind? Little decisions we make along the way may not seem important, but cumulatively they formulate our character and impact those around us. Before acting, we need to remember what others would say in our eulogy.

In our work lives, it can be tempting to get ahead by misrepresenting our product or offering advice that is not in the best interests of our client. We may get a short-term win in the form of a new client or a big sale. But do we want someone retelling that story to our grandchildren at our funeral? We may be too focused on our own career to mentor a new employee or to help a struggling colleague. Is that the legacy we want to leave with our organization?

In our personal lives, financial struggles and other pressures can sap our energy and take our attention and focus away from our spouse or children. It is important to work hard and build the best life possible. But at our funeral, no one is going to talk about the size of our house or the number of cars we kept in the garage.

In the end, our family relationships and close friends will be all that matter. We must keep that long-term perspective in mind while fighting the tumultuous storms of the present. We have an opportunity to positively impact so many lives through our actions. We need to treat our clients with respect and dignity. We need to mentor a colleague so they can flourish in their new role. (After all, somebody helped *us* along our own journey.) Most importantly, we need to work hard without losing sight of our close relationships with friends and family. These will form our legacy.

But what happens if we make a mistake along the way? Will we be vilified at our own funeral? Of course not! Nobody is perfect, and we should not expect this of others or ourselves. At some point, we are bound to stumble. Do not despair. We will be judged more for how we respond to our mistakes. Did we take responsibility for our actions and apologize? Did we learn from the incident and ensure it will never happen again? Did we gain valuable appreciation and an understanding of how lucky we are to have friends and family help us through the difficult times? These setbacks can define our life even more than our greatest triumphs.

Stepping up and taking responsibility is one of the most courageous things we can do. Embracing the teachable moment by not allowing it to happen again is the definition of character. We need to use these stumbling blocks as an opportunity to create an inspirational, redemptive legacy. As long as our setbacks do not impact our close relationships, they will be a blip on the radar of our life.

We were not put on this earth to live small. We will work hard, dream big, love deeply and create an extraordinary life. But we need to maintain appreciation along the way. Financial security is important, but we cannot jeopardize our relationships to achieve this. If we maintain healthy, loving relationships, we have lived an extraordinary life. If we help and mentor our colleagues, friends, and family, we have lived an extraordinary life. If we make some mistakes along the way, but take ownership and responsibility for our actions, we have lived an extraordinary life. Before acting, we need to think about what people would say at our funeral. This principle should guide our actions and impact our decisions. Our close family and friends will be there for us in the end.

We need to start living our own epic eulogy in the present!

WHAT IS YOUR *THING?*

"Rockets are cool. There's just no getting around that."
—Elon Musk

Every legendary figure has their special "thing." Some defining characteristic, unique talent or incredible vision that propels them to greatness. George Lucas has the amazing ability to devise memorable characters and create new worlds. Muhammad Ali could float like a butterfly and sting like a bee. Elon Musk has the simple yet powerful vision to innovate and make space travel accessible to the masses. These figures all leveraged their unique qualities to create a great American legacy that will endure for generations. If only we had that type of special talent. If only we could make that kind of impact on this world.

But the fact is that *everyone* has their special *thing*. Some hidden talent, quirky ritual, or endearing quality that contributes to their unique character. They may never appear on the cover of *Time Magazine*, but they are no less influential in their local circles. I have one friend who passes out Christmas wreath stickers everywhere he goes during the holidays. *Who doesn't get a kick out of that?* Another friend's father walks around with silver dollar coins and pulls them "out of the ear" of bewildered children. *Classic!* Still another friend makes sandwiches and passes them out to unsuspecting homeless people throughout the city. *Now that is making a difference!*

Your *thing* could be much simpler. A snorting laugh (you know who you are), an oft-repeated tagline ("Let's roll, dawgs!"), a slightly annoying yet somehow endearing habit (fist bump!), or a fanatic allegiance to a team (Is that guy really wearing a Babe Laufenberg jersey?). These quirky qualities are not necessarily prerequisites for fame and fortune. They may not get us into an Ivy League school or ensure a job in the corner office. But they represent genuine personality and understated charm that make us unique and memorable. All of those qualities bring a little bit of joy to a small corner of the community and, collectively, help make this world a better place. We should all take the time to appreciate these qualities and these people.

But issues can arise when we suffer a setback and begin to feel less confident about our standing in the world. We question our quirky, unique qualities and wonder why we can't be like everyone else. We start focusing more on conformity and less on our true personality. If we can think more strategically and less emotionally, maybe the client will take notice. If we ditch our American flag tie and white shoes for a blue blazer and loafers, maybe management will take us more seriously. If we stop playing with reckless abandon on the athletic field and stay under control, maybe we will gain more favor from the coach. Maybe.

But emotion might be your *thing*. Those white "Uncle Eddie" shoes might be your *thing*. Playing like a mad dog might be your *thing*. Our quirks and our idiosyncrasies may handicap us at various points in our life. But that is our *authentic* nature. That is the unique charm and talent we are bringing into this world. We cannot hide from it. We should not *want* to hide from it.

Our special talents and personality will get us back on our feet in troubled times. Let someone else worry about being "perfect." Let someone else worry about trying to impress the mainstream. We need to stay true to our character and embrace the *thing* that makes us unique! That will fuel our resilience!

So go ahead and send out that way-too-long and way-too-personal holiday card every year. Go ahead and salute every time you pass someone in the hallway. Go ahead and play an entire round of golf with only a putter. Our *thing* has gotten us this far in life. We need to stick with it in the difficult times. We need to stick with it when no one seems to have our back. We may not realize it, but the world is starving for our own unique and endearing qualities.

Let's go ahead and do our thing!

WHO ARE THE "GO-TO" PEOPLE IN YOUR LIFE?

"A friend in need is a friend indeed."
—English Proverb

March is a particularly special time to be a college basketball fan. The best basketball teams in the country battle for one championship trophy over a three-week period during "March Madness." In the close games, there is one player who has the ball in his hands as the clock winds down. The team relies on this leader to determine the entire fate of the season. All the pressure is on this player, and he *wants* to take the shot with the game on the line. He assumes the risk, shakes off the pressure and has the chance to become an instant legend (if only for a moment) by sticking the buzzer-beater. Christian Laettner from Duke. Bryce Drew from Valparaiso. Kris Jenkins from Villanova. These players became legends and the poster children for the "go-to" guys of March.

As in basketball, each one of us has a "go-to" person we rely on when the pressure is intense. In business, it could be the trustworthy salesperson who calmly explains the benefits of a solution to a doubting client. Or the visionary CEO who can close a crumbling deal with sheer passion. Or the even-keeled manager who removes all the internal roadblocks for his team members. These people make us feel comfortable when the deal is on the line and the business is at a crossroads. Placing our trust in them usually ensures victory.

In the same manner, each of us has a go-to person in our personal lives. Perhaps it is a spouse, a parent, a family member, a close friend or some combination of all of these. We trust these people with our deepest secrets and turn to them in both the good times and the bad. Our go-to person accepts the pressure, welcomes our problems, and *wants* us to succeed. We simply could not make it without their support.

It is in times of crisis when we need our go-to people the most! If we strive for resilience and want to move forward, we cannot do it alone. Resilience requires teamwork. If we are struggling with a sale, we can't be afraid to involve our trusted leaders to help guide us through the process. If we are struggling with a complex concept in or out of the classroom, we can't be resistant to involving a mentor or advisor to help guide us through the difficult period. If we are struggling with leadership and direction in our company, it's time to find your savviest business contact and seek out their advice. These people will help us in crunch time and ensure we are always on the winning team.

It is even more important to find the go-to person in our personal lives. We all experience setbacks and bumps in the road at some point in our journey. *Financial difficulty. Relationship problems. Legal issues. Academic stress or heartache.* Everyone needs a go-to person in times of distress or despair. We trust their advice, and they can help us move forward even if they are only in "listen mode." Just confiding in this person instills us with hope and allows us to face our issues with confidence. These go-to people are the MVPs in our own lives!

It is also important to remember that we need to *be* that go-to person for others. Resilience is not a one-way street. We must listen to the problems of those closest to us. And look for warning signs when someone we care about may be in trouble. We need to be a shining example of integrity in our personal and professional lives and let our inner circle know we will always be there for them. Just as we need that go-to person in difficult times, there is someone who needs our support in return. And being there for others will give us the strength to persevere when we face our own difficult moments. Providing this go-to support will embolden us when our own support system breaks down.

But what happens when our go-to person can no longer help us? We may lose a spouse, parent or close friend to illness or old age. While incredibly painful, giving up is not an option. It is now our turn to be strong and step into the starting lineup! We need to channel our support into helping others. We need to set an example and be the rock for our own children and loved ones during their difficult times. Being a go-to person is about paying it forward. We need to channel the support we have received into helping our own circle of family and friends. This will be our legacy.

Everyone needs that "go-to" person in their lives. We must appreciate all that they do for us. And we must honor them by paying that support forward. Stay resilient. *And be that go-to person for others!*

NOURISHMENT AND THE PUSHY WEDDING CATERER

"Give to yourself as much as you give of yourself."
—Suze Orman

There are certain moments in our lives we never forget. Perhaps a particular play from a game in our youth. Perhaps an early memory of a parent that still warms our heart. Perhaps a special moment on vacation, or a personal connection that made a difference. The memories don't have to be life-changing or even significant. But for some reason, they stay emblazoned in living color on our brains.

One such memory occurred at our wedding (many, many years ago!). It was a glorious affair, full of family and great friends. What an incredible opportunity to have everyone we cared about gathered in one spot for a celebration.

Naturally, we were busy going from table to table, shaking hands, checking in, and making sure everyone was having a good time. And along the way, we had the cake cutting, the toast (great job, Steve!) and all the other ceremonies that go along with the whirlwind day.

About halfway through the reception, our caterer came up to us and *insisted* that we eat. We were both caught in an impromptu receiving line and didn't have time to break away.

"Don't make me drag you away," the caterer insisted, only half kidding.

Above our mild protests, the caterer grabbed both of us by the arm and marched us out of the reception hall. Just beyond the door was a table set for two with huge plates of pasta. Neither one of us thought we were hungry. But after the first forkful, both of our plates were cleaned in seconds! We were both starving. But we were too caught up in adrenaline, excitement and chaos to recognize how badly we needed nourishment.

And I think a lot of us fall into that same trap in our work and personal lives.

In our work lives, we can get consumed by the minutiae of our everyday responsibilities. There are people to manage, goals to hit, problems to solve, and projects to deliver. And the technology and competition are moving faster than we ever thought possible. We can go entire weeks laboring to scratch items off our to-do list in a futile effort to stay ahead.

But how many times do we step back and ask bigger questions? *What are my high-level goals? What are my priorities? How am I taking care of myself so I can achieve success?* There is a difference between being busy and being productive. Sometimes, we need to step back from the chaos of the day-to-day and assess where we are in our careers. We need to step off the wheel and give ourselves the proper nourishment of perspective and appreciation. Only when we take a break do we realize how much we need it!

And the same is true in our personal lives. It is very easy to get caught up in myriad social functions and obligations. We have commitments, outings and activities that fill in any remaining "free" time. Our lives can toggle between the blurred lines of family, friends, and coworkers.

For the most part, this is healthy and it certainly beats loneliness and isolation. But how many times do we step back and assess our actions? *Are all of our activities necessary and productive? Are all of our relationships healthy and affirming? Have we taken any time to ensure our needs are met in the process?* It is right and responsible to take care of others and bring joy and fulfilment to family and friends. But we have to make sure we take care of ourselves along the way. *Nourishment starts from within.*

Why is this so important? Without this nourishment and perspective, it is MUCH more difficult to stay resilient when the walls start to crumble. In times of strife and uncertainty, we need to stay focused. We need to be strong. We need all of our energy centered on getting back to our best selves. If we get caught up in the adrenaline and chaos of our everyday lives, we will find ourselves hungry and weak when we need it most. We need to feed ourselves before we get to that point.

And we need people to help us realize the depth of our hunger. Who are the "caterers" in your life? Who provides encouragement and nourishment? Who helps you appreciate all you have in this world? Cherish these people. Let them help you. Do not shut them out. They may seem pushy or intrusive at times. But sometimes we need other people to help us see what we can't see ourselves.

And don't forget to check on yourself. We all need to take some time away from the madness. It is okay to give yourself a break. That appreciation and nourishment will ultimately feed your resilience.

GUARDIAN ANGELS AND THE POWER OF RESILIENCE

"I knew he wouldn't die, because his life was like the roots of a tree that went miles into the soil and miles around its trunk. A tree that big can never die."
—Donald Miller, *A Million Miles in a Thousand Years*

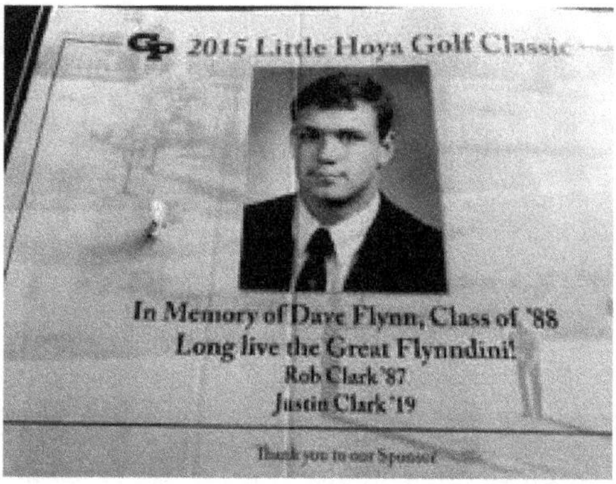

My daughter Courtney loves to decorate for Christmas. And I love that about her. She will dive into the box of lights, grab some tape and thumbtacks, and string them throughout the house. One Christmas, she was hanging some lights in the basement when the tape gave way and the strand dropped to the ground. One of the bulbs next to the outlet broke upon impact. And just above the outlet was a poster of Dave Flynn.

Dave Flynn was a good friend who passed away unexpectedly and tragically several years ago. He was a larger-than-life character with a larger-than-life heart. If you were with Dave, you were in for a good time. And you were always protected. He had a way of making you feel that *all was right with the world*. So I have kept that old golf tournament poster in my basement to remind our family of that feeling of safety.

Courtney reached out to replace the broken bulb, not realizing the lights were still plugged in. As her fingers were inches from the socket, a giant spark shot out and went straight to the poster (instead of toward Courtney), causing a mini explosion. Courtney immediately pulled back from the lights. The back of the poster was burned. It could have been Courtney. She snapped back into it and unplugged the lights. Everyone was safe.

Could there be a scientific explanation? Could it be a coincidence? Or was she saved by a guardian angel?

All scenarios are possible. But I choose to believe we have people looking out for us in this world. And couldn't we all use the extra help?

Our lives are not easy. There are challenges and pitfalls at every turn. We struggle for financial security. We search for meaning and motivation in our work lives. We worry about keeping our children safe. We battle with strong personalities in our work and personal lives. We have to overcome more challenges than we ever dreamed possible. There are times when we feel all alone in this struggle. There are times when we do not have the energy to move forward. But stagnation and resignation are not options.

What will get us moving? What will inspire us in these darker times? It could come from anywhere. A soulful song. A reflective book. An act of mercy. Encouraging words from a friend. *A spark from a poster!* The motivation is all around us. But we have to be *open* to it. We have to believe things will get better. We have to believe we are not alone in this world.

We won't be able to recover if we put up walls and retreat into our shell. We can choose to ignore the signs. We can focus on the science and ignore the faith. We can believe in coincidences and dismiss guardian angels. We can stand alone against the rising tide of despair. But we do so at our own peril.

Resilience is a team sport. There are times when even the strongest individuals are no match for the challenges that lie ahead. There are times when we need to look externally for support and motivation. We won't be able to do it alone. We *need* our close circle of family and friends. We need them to help us stay resilient!

But resilience itself doesn't make any logical sense. Why subject ourselves to any more heartbreak or loss? Why not retreat and cut our losses? Because we owe it to our friends. We owe it to our family. We owe it to anyone who has ever believed in us. We owe it to all those in our inner circle who have gone before us.

There are certain individuals who will never leave us. *A parent, a child, a sibling, a spouse, a friend, a loved one.* They may leave this world, but their influence, their advice, and their genuine care will live on forever. We can see them working through the people they have left behind. We can see them in our everyday lives. *They will always be with us.*

And if we have the faith and truly believe we are not alone, there is nothing we can't overcome. There is nothing that will hold us back.

I believe we can't explain everything in this world through science or coincidence. I believe in guardian angels and the power of resilience. *I believe that some people will never die.*

AVOIDING THE CRAB MENTALITY

"Keep away from people who belittle your ambitions. Small people always do that, but the really great make you feel that you, too, can become great."
—Mark Twain

To lead a resilient life, we must summon the courage to shake the "crab mentality." This refers to crabs in a pot of boiling water that constantly pull one another back down in a pointless "king of the hill" competition. As soon as one crab is about to escape, another drags him back down to the bottom of the pot. Instead of helping each other out, this mentality ensures the collective demise of the group. Essentially, it is the ultimate manifestation of the "If I can't have it, neither can you" philosophy. This flies in the face of everyday resilience!

In our work lives, how often do we root for another to succeed? Do we appreciate it when a fellow salesperson brings in a big deal, or do we belittle their accomplishment? Do we try to help a new team member get up to speed as quickly as possible, or do we angle to impede his or her progress? As managers, do we foster the collective success of our team, or do we sabotage those team members who can possibly take our job? Do we encourage freethinking, or do we take credit for a team member's idea just to keep them at the bottom of the pot?

The most dynamic work cultures encourage the success of the team by promoting and genuinely rooting for the individuals to succeed. There is no tolerance for the crab mentality, even if it means letting one get out of the pot. Instead of forcing a successful member to stay, a positive work culture encourages growth and views a promotion (both internal and external) as the ultimate form of flattery.

In our personal life, are we happy when someone buys a larger house, or do we find a way to turn a positive into a negative? ("Do they really need *that* much space?") Are we happy when a friend finally finds a suitable partner, or do we nitpick about the shortcomings of their new spouse? ("Did you see his hair? Comb-over!") Are we supportive when a member of our inner circle achieves financial freedom, or do we question the legitimacy of their success? ("Yeah, they make a lot of money, but that is such unfulfilling work!"). Belittling their success only serves as a roadblock to our own development and happiness.

Instead of pulling them down to the bottom of the pot, be happy for their accomplishments. Let it serve as motivation for our own future success. Someone else has blazed a path to glory. Now we know it is possible. If they can do it, so can we!

But this crab mentality is especially damaging when we suffer a setback in our life. During these difficult times, the success of others exacerbates our own undesirable situation. Misery and jealousy violently collide, and we want everyone to feel our pain. This creates a vicious circle of despair and self-loathing. It becomes much more difficult to move forward toward resilience if we are looking for fault and failure in everything around us. Ironically, celebrating the accomplishments of others, especially those in our inner circle, can help pull us out of the boiling pot!

Instead of the "If I can't have it, neither can you" philosophy, celebrate the "If I can't have it, I'm glad someone I care about *can*" philosophy. That healthy mindset will allow us to move forward with our own shortcomings and setbacks. It will create a stronger, more vibrant team at work. It will create a more loving environment in our personal life. It will allow us to escape the boiling pot of negative thinking and move forward toward personal freedom.

A pot of boiling crabs does not have to be a metaphor for our life. We need to focus on our own journey to success and happiness. When we get there, we need to realize that others may still be suffering. Let's reach back down and lend them a helping hand (or claw!). Some will still try to pull us back down into the boiling pot. We don't have time for them. We will be too busy celebrating the accomplishments of others. We will be too busy inspiring others to succeed. We will be too busy leading the resilient and healthy lifestyle we were destined to live!

BE PRESENT IN THE PRESENT

"Happiness is not something you postpone for the future; it is something you enjoy in the present."
—Jim Rohn

Life can spin out of control with the stress of work and the increasing stress of family life. We rarely have the time or energy for reflection and appreciation. Instead, we race from task to task, and conversation to conversation, trying to keep up with an endless stream of demands on our time. Or, worse, we dwell on the mistakes of the past and become paralyzed by our failures. The ability to maintain perspective and appreciation in the present moment will allow us to better focus on a future task and move forward. In short, we must recognize the importance of being present in the present!

In good times, we must enjoy the moment and recognize that something special is happening. I still remember the feeling of walking off the field in my last high school football game at Georgetown Prep. As referenced earlier in the book, we had a very special team and ended the season undefeated and highly ranked. I recognized in the present that this was a moment I would look back on fondly in the future. I slowly walked off the field and soaked in every detail and emotion of the moment. I remember the look on my parents' faces as they cheered from the stands. I remember my teammates celebrating both individually and together. I remember the smell of the grass and mud and the long shadows over the scoreboard. Everything was happening in slow motion as I reveled in the moment.

Because I was present in the present, the memory of that single moment has lasted a lifetime. Too often, we don't appreciate what we have in the moment, and it is only in retrospect we recognize the significance of the event. Happiness should not be experienced in the rearview mirror! Let's take the time to reflect on the present and be thankful for the current blessings in our life.

It seems reasonable to recognize and appreciate the present when the good times are rolling. But what about "being present in the present" during the down times? While not as easy, it is every bit as important. If we are going to lead a resilient life, we have to recognize and appreciate those challenging moments as well. There is more to being present in the present than yearning for better times. It reminds me of a classic saying in the military, which many soldiers remember during battle: "Never assume that things can't get worse."

At work, if we lose a big sale, remember there are other clients and other opportunities. If we don't recognize the present and take action, we may lose them all! If we miss an assignment, recognize it, but don't dwell on it forever. That will only lead to more mistakes in the future. We need to embrace the present failure and take control of our future. Remember, everyday resilience is about moving forward!

Living in the present, whether in good times or in bad times, can help us better appreciate our lives and help us achieve peace and happiness. As we near the end of this book, *the best present I can present to you is the importance of being present in the present!*

EVERYDAY RESILIENCE PROFILE ON APPRECIATION: COACH ROOSTER NALLS AND HIS FIVE LIFE LESSONS

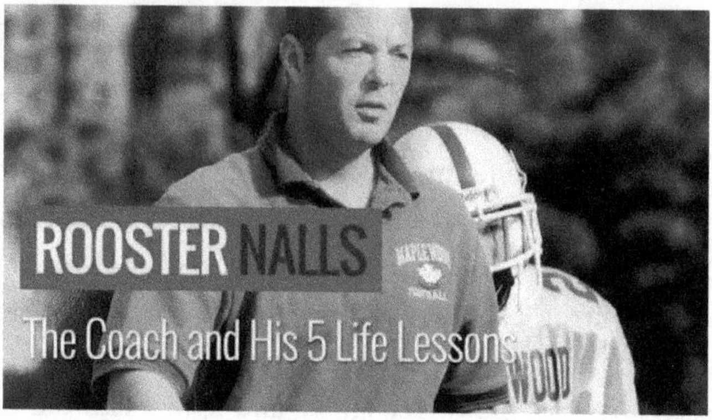

He is a husband and the father of three beautiful children. Generations of players at Maplewood, a youth football team in the Washington, DC, area, have embraced his passion and fire. He has mentored and placed dozens of coaches in other jobs. He is a local legend.

He grew up the youngest of eight brothers in a large Catholic family in Bethesda, Maryland. As is customary in such tight-knit families, the older siblings appointed nicknames to the younger siblings. Names such as "Stretch," "Toot," and "Whales" might as well have been printed on their birth certificates. What name did they save for their youngest brother, Joseph? "Rooster" Nalls!

Rooster Nalls has been coaching youth football for twenty-five years.

For Rooster, coaching is something he appreciates as much as *breathing*. It also involves a constant search for improvement. After every game, *win or lose*, he devises schemes to make his team better. But more than anything, he wants his boys to understand the fundamentals of building a successful team. And, just as critical, he wants them to carry these lessons away from the football field and into their adult lives.

At the beginning of each season, Rooster instills these fundamentals in a series of impassioned speeches to his team. Bite-sized nuggets of inspiration that form the backbone of a cohesive unit. Words of wisdom that serve his players far beyond the game of football. At their core, these lessons focus on **appreciation**. Each lesson is as important as the next:

Hit**
Have Fun
Put the Team First
Pay the Price
Play with Pride
**Hitting also ends the list. Because it "begins and ends with hitting!"

These fundamentals apply to the game of football. These fundamentals apply to the game of life.

For Coach Nalls, *hitting* is about more than just strapping on your helmet and running into someone. It is the ultimate expression of self-confidence. It is a willingness to trust yourself completely.

"Initiating contact is a sign that you have let go of your fears and have *committed* to the team. When a player makes the decision to step up and deliver a hit, they have made the decision to go 'all in.' It all begins with hitting!"

In the same way, we can't just sit back and let life wash over us. We must initiate the contact. We must overcome our fears and confidently pursue our dreams and goals. Sometimes, that means believing we will be successful even in the face of defeat. We only get one shot at this life. We must *commit* ourselves to excellence. Either we are all in, or we sit on the sidelines!

Having fun is the hallmark of a Coach Nalls team. But this is not about messing around in practice and making jokes.

"Having fun means playing with energy. Having fun means playing with emotion. When a player makes the choice to have fun (and it is a choice!), everyone on the team feeds off this spirit. The players put in so much work. If they aren't having fun, why bother?"

In the same way, we must *choose* to have fun in our own lives. We need to embrace our work challenges and attack them with energy. We need to throw ourselves into our relationships and openly express our emotion. We need to be that shining example that inspires people to keep moving forward. Having fun is a choice. And it is a choice that can have an enormous impact on all those around us.

Life is full of hard work and difficult challenges. But if we approach them with energy and enthusiasm, we will have a lot of fun along the way!

But it is all about *putting the team first.* This is critical in the game of football. And, as Coach Nalls preaches, *it is simple, but not easy.*

It is not easy because we all have egos. We all want to catch the pass. We all want to score the touchdown. We all want to hear the cheers from the crowds.

"But putting the team first means everyone understands their role. Each role is hugely important to the overall success of the team. No *one* player is above the rest. When the crowd cheers, they are cheering for the team!"

In the same way, the best managers put the interests of their team above their own needs. They know that by sharing the spotlight and helping their team members succeed, the company will be stronger in the end.

Loving parents know that their family is the most important team. It is not about their individual glory or success. A healthy, functional family starts at the top and is the ultimate reward.

We all must cast our egos aside and put our teams first. That is the sign of a true champion!

But at some point, you must *pay the price.* Having success on the football field is not about just showing up. Coach Nalls demands *maximum* effort. The work you put in during the sticky months of August will pay dividends down the line.

"Everything worthwhile requires sacrifice and effort. If you want to win a championship, you gotta pay the price!"

For the rest of us, we can't just go through the motions in our own lives and expect to achieve greatness. Life is not about just showing up. We must put in long hours. We must demonstrate maximum effort. We must be willing to put ourselves out there and suffer ridicule and defeat.

The road to success is not easy. It will take courage and grit. There will be dark times and down moments. But if we pay the price and never stop believing, we will win out in the end!

Finally, you have to *play with pride*. As Coach Nalls says,

"You have to care so much, it's stupid! That starts with the little things. Take pride in your uniform. Take pride in the pre-game drills. Take pride in showing up on time."

That pride carries over into the games where his players take pride in playing for one another.

"If everyone is playing with pride, the team will maximize its potential. And, win or lose, the players can hold their heads high!"

In the same way, we must take pride in everything we do in our work and personal lives. The menial tasks. The seemingly insignificant assignments. The mundane errands. We can't pick and choose what we approach with pride.

This pride must shine through in every facet of our lives. Our relationships. Our family. Our career. Our hobbies. We have to care so much, it's stupid! Because when we do, we lead by example. We inspire others to be better. And we proclaim to the world that *pride still matters*!

Every season, Coach Nalls takes his players on a journey. Over the years, he has inspired an entire generation through his appreciation of the game and commitment to excellence. How long can he continue to coach? Is there an end in sight?

"I'll stop coaching when football isn't the only thing I think about when I'm there."

Amen. And thank you for providing the final lesson. **When you are fiercely dedicated to a cause, there is nothing that can distract you from your goals.** When you are coaching, you coach with passion. When you are playing, you play with reckless abandon. When you are working, you dedicate yourself to the task at hand. And when you are spending time with your family, *you spend time with your family.*

You cannot be physically in one place, and mentally in another. Regardless of what you are doing, you have to care so much, it's stupid!

Take life head-on!

Have fun with it!

Put your team first!

Pay the price!

Execute with pride!

And, finally, stay focused and appreciate every second you are out on the field.

Coach Rooster Nalls has provided a guideline for leading a resilient life. It is simple. But it is not easy.

We all have this game plan inside of us.

Now let's all go out and make the world a better place!

THE FINAL WORD

"Success is not final, failure is not fatal: it is the courage to continue that counts."
—Winston Churchill

Our life is a constant journey. There will be incredible moments of unbridled joy. There will be devastating moments of anguish and despair. There will be times when, despite our best plans, we have little control over our situation. Rarely do we have an easy path. But how we react during those down moments will shape our character and establish our grit.

We have a choice. We can mentally give up, abandon our dreams and live our life without ever reaching our potential. We can remain bitter, act like a victim, and constantly complain about our circumstances. Or we can *choose* to be resilient.

Resilience leads to a path of happiness and success. Resilience builds our confidence and allows us to tackle our fears and doubts. Resilience enhances our relationships and allows us to overcome any obstacle.

And, through the pages of this book, we have seen how choosing resilience enables us to overcome **adversity**, maintain a healthy **perspective**, fuel our **passion**, and experience deep, heart-felt **appreciation**.

And now for the best part. We don't need to be rich and famous to be resilient. We don't need to be superstars to be resilient. We all face challenges and struggles in our everyday lives. And we ALL have the ability to overcome these difficult times through our own actions!

This everyday resilience dwells in each one of us. It is my hope that this book serves as a catalyst for all of us to find our inner strength, to keep moving forward and to be a positive influence in this world.

Thank you for spending time on this quest for everyday resilience. We must strive for resilience in our professional lives. We must strive for resilience in our personal lives. But achieving this resilience will not be a linear journey. Feel free to refer back to certain chapters or messages as you move forward with your lives. Whether in good times or in bad, we all need a simple guide to help us get back on the right path and find our way. We all deserve success and happiness. We all deserve to be everyday heroes in our own lives.

Good luck with your own personal journey, and don't forget to keep smiling along the way!

THE END

Find out more about Rob on his blog at www.resilientworker.com.

CPSIA information can be obtained
at www.ICGtesting.com
Printed in the USA
LVHW090919100920
665516LV00009B/98

9 781646 630271

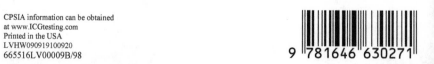